Sri Lankan Dessert

FAKHRI

Copyright © 2012 Fakhri

All rights reserved.

ISBN: 0615577458
ISBN-13: 978-0615577456

DEDICATION

To all my near and dear friends and colleagues from N.E.D. who liked my writings and persuaded me to publish them.

Thank You!

TABLE OF CONTENTS

	Preface	Pg 4
1	Aap Ka Yeh Hafta Kaisa Guzray Ga	Pg 5
2	Aap Ki Kameeni	Pg 8
3	ASI Shafiqullah Niazi	Pg 12
4	Asian Whatever	Pg 18
5	Badi Mushkil Hay	Pg 22
6	Busharraf's Campaign Speech	Pg 25
7	Chief justice Bahal Ho Gaye Hain	Pg 29
8	Choroo Buddhay	Pg 31
9	Exotic Dishes	Pg 34
10	Fasad Fi Sabilillah	Pg 37
11	Fudget	Pg 39
12	Ghaban Ka Chakka Laga	Pg 43
13	Ghareeb Nay Pait Bhar Kar Roti Khaali	Pg 45
14	Girgit Team Lineup	Pg 48
15	Hellucinations	Pg 49
16	Illactions	Pg 52
17	Karachi Flavors	Pg 56

18	Kuch Na Samjhay Khuda Karay Koi	Pg 59
19	Mahawaray Shahawaray	Pg 62
20	Main	Pg 65
21	Masael Aur Un Pay Hull	Pg 68
22	Maths 101	Pg 73
23	National Bank of Pakistan – Main Branch	Pg 78
24	New Ministries	Pg 84
25	Nishan-e-Gather	Pg 87
26	One Good News	Pg 90
27	Pakistani Innovations	Pg 94
28	Poly-Tickelly Incorrect	Pg 97
29	Saeen Munhjo NRO	Pg 101
30	Secular Phones	Pg 103
31	Shaheed-e-Business	Pg 105
32	Some Useful Innovations	Pg 109
33	Sri Lankan Dessert	Pg 114
34	Tussi Arahay Ho Kay Ja Rahay Ho	Pg 118
35	United Islam	Pg 123
36	Zaroorat-e-Jahez	Pg 127

PREFACE

Being a software engineer, sometimes life looked like a bunch of algorithms. One gets executed after the other, sort of mechanically, boring to say the least.

Since I left my beloved Pakistan and my city, Karachi, I started looking at life in a realistic way. And I realized that life is far from boring...it is the most amazing thing in the realms of this universe. And life in Pakistan, well, it's actually something out of this universe.

Instead of having a cheeky attitude to what is not right and why is it so...I felt these serious topics to be a divine comedy. These writings started as a few mail postings, but became habitual for me over time. With a little appreciation from friends, I decided to compile it all in one book.

Sure, we can attempt to change things...but for now, let's change the way we look at them!

Sri Lankan Dessert

AAP KA YEH HAFTA KAISA GUZRAY GA

Kiyon Kay Pichla Hafta Jaisa Guzarta Hay...Agla Hafta Waisa Hi Guzray Ga!

MONDAY: Venus will be in the 6th house of Sun where she will get pregnant. Actually the Sun tried to woo poor Venus by saying "Ayee Na Aap Hamaray Ghar!" Although she said "Naa Padosi Naa!", Venus eventually got attracted by Sun's grave gravity.

A pregnant Venus will cause mood swings on Libra and Gemini zodiacs. Nausea, fatigue, and loss of appetite will be common with frequent trips to the washroom. Quarreling with the partner and threats of telling everyone everything could increase. Buying cheap calling cards for the domestic partner so they can talk to "Amma-Abba" and investing in a $25 gift certificate should compensate for the "pregnant Venus effects". For folks in Pakistan, sending the spouse to "Susrael" (Kharadar, Karimabad etc.) will soothe things down.

TUESDAY: Today, a Full Moon will start showing its affects. A close friend may make fun of your full moon in a gathering. Calling him names will have no effect as everyone will be laughing only at you.

For folks with Sagittarius and Leo signs, it's time to invest in a decent hair-transplant. Also, folks from Cancer and Pisces signs, you may want to check out Laser eye surgery and liposuction. Friends from Virgo may settle only with wrinkle free creams. Friends from Capricorn & Aquarius, today is the day to choose between hair transplant and valve transplant.

WEDNESAY: Oye Hoye! Jupiter is at odds with Mars over the corner house while Mercury is wooing Saturn for the ground floor condo. Losing your mobile phone while saving your life will enhance your spirituality and make you feel humble. This opportunity can be viewed as a time to buy your 15th mobile this year. Also, there will be increased trips to "Baba Ji's" grave for Fateha and slaughtering a black goat.

Folks in the US will feel high-spirited after dodging the IRS and saving tax money only to find out that they still can't afford to pay for car gas. Intelligent people will view this opportunity to invest in a bicycle.

THURSDAY: Pluto has gone lost in the sky while Ur-anus is positioned dangerously. Trying to go to "Aisi Waisi" websites at work will finally bring its consequences. After you get caught "blue-handed", the manager may come looking for you.

By telling your manager more about such websites, you will find a trusted and well-wishing friend in your boss. Getting caught inside your home is, however, a different story. Your six year old can be found praying on Friday "Ya Allah! Un Saari Ghareeb Bachiyon Ko Kapray Pahnaday Jo Meray Abbu Kay Computer Main Hain!"

FRIDAY: The sun will be hot and the moon will be cold. While you are anticipating the weekend, suddenly Maulvi Sahib will tell you how disgusting this world is especially your own. This logic can be used to try to persuade the spouse that a new car or house furniture is worthless while a true loving husband is priceless.

Friends from Aries & Taurus can use Friday to find coupons for "Where Kids eat free!" while folks from Scorpio need to tell the visiting relatives that kids are sick and this month doesn't look good for a visitation.

SATURDAY: The weekly call to Pakistan will reveal that your three brothers-in-law are out of work since they can't find a job that suits "their" caliber. Intelligent folks will immediately start planning to apply for US/Canadian visas for these bored in-laws.

Trying not to apply for immigration will not only cause havoc in the planetary system but the person will be able to see most of the planets by his own naked eye. This may also cause the person to be ejected from his own house. In that case, investing in a sleeping bag will be a good advice. This applies to all zodiac signs.

SUNDAY: Saturn has entered "Sarh-Satti" which will cause "Lag Gai Batti" for all concerned people. Today, a relaxed web browsing session will be interrupted by grocery shopping. Someone with the name starting with "Bay" can be irritating. Someone with the name of "Kaaf/Gaaf" will bring weird news and also their will be problems from "Laam", "Meem", and "Noon". All confidential things and personal secrets that you had told "Chay", will be found on internet.

At the time when a dreadful Monday is looking straight into the eyes, buying some thing for yourself more expensive than $3.49 or Rs. 275, will help you feel elevated and high-spirited.

AAP KI KAMEENI

It was the early 90's and I was studying in New York. My friend, who was studying with me, was one of the developers of an Urdu Desktop publishing system. The software was bought by a local Pakistani community newspaper, with Mr. Javed Minhas of Rawalpindi as the chief editor.

They were looking for an Urdu composer at that time and they couldn't find one. My friend had agreed to help them with composing the weekly newspaper until they find a full-time person. One such week, he got sick right on Friday, which was the final day for publishing of the weekly.

He requested me to go and help them out since I could type Urdu scripts. He said that he is using a new Nastaaleeq 12 font which is quite exotic, but it's not a true type font and has not been fully calibrated on HP laser printer. The editor Sahib loves it and what he does not love is arguing. According to him, just a little work was left and I would be done in a few hours. That day, I had an exam which would be finished by 10:00 at night. I asked another friend to be there just to make the editor feel that help is on its way until I come.

Sri Lankan Dessert

By the time I got to the newspaper office in Midtown Manhattan, my friend had printed the main headline and the main news body and was showing it to me. He looked sleepy as it was passed 11:00. I pasted the news with the header and was about to show it to the editor – Mr. Javed Minhas, when I suddenly looked at the beautiful size 18 white on black headlines: "Nawaz Shareef Ka Benazir Ko Jawab: Mazay Ki Raat Apni Jagah, Qanooni Karrawaai Apni Jagah". I looked at the original script, "Nawaz Shareef Ka Benazir Ko Jawab: Mazakirat Apni Jagah, Qanooni Karrawai Apni Jagah". I tried to explain to him that I could become Shaheed in no time, if this would publish.

He was too sleepy and grumpy by now - "Khood Fix Kar Lo". Anyway, I thanked him and took the driving seat. The first thing – both Shift Keys on the keyboard were not working. I told Javed Sahib that the Shift Key is not working. He retorted, "Jadoon Chal Si Tay Don't Worry!"

OK, I typed a news from a piece of paper about the navy foiling a smuggling attempt involving a launch, and then started proof reading:

"Pakistani Navy Nay Al-Zulfiqar Tanzeem Ki Qeemti Lunch Smuggle Karnay Ki Koshish Nakaam Bana Di. Bakhabar Zaraye Kay Mutabiq Aaj 3:00 Bajay Al-Zulfiqar Nay Aik Lunch Jis Main Kaafi Qeemti Ashiya Thi, Dubai Layjani Ki Koshish Ki. Jis Par Navy Nay Karrawai Kartay Huay Order Diya Kay Lunch Hamaray Hawalay Kardo. Al-Zulfiqar Nay Kaha Kay Hum Lunch Dubo Dayn Gay Magar Hawaalay Nahin Karayngay. Is Par Navy Nay Lunch Qabzay Main Lay Kay Khood Istemaal Karna Shuroo Kardia!"

The 'Laam-Alif' which was 'Shift-L' was typing as just 'Laam'. I looked around the office and found an old keyboard being used as a door stopper. I plugged it in. Voila! The Shift Key started working…although now all the keys started making noises. As soon as I finished typing half a page, Javed Sahib retorted, "Oye Fakhri

Bhai…Tussaan Tay Khaber Mail Wich Bayh Gaye Ho!" I explained to him the circumstances and he looked a bit relaxed, "Jadoon Chal Si Tay Don't Worry!"

When Mr. Javed Minhas used to laugh, it sounded like a heavy carton being dragged on a mosaic floor, although by now I had started liking him a bit. He handed me a piece of paper as the next news item. The one-liner was for a company fund raising, "Sub Apnay Fund Miss Naheed Kay Paas Jama Kara Dain". I used the new Nastaleeq 12 font and printed it. The noise of the printer got merged with the noise of a carton being dragged. And this time, an amused, "Jadoon Chal Si Tay Don't Worry! Kasme Khuda Di!"

I went to where he was sitting and he joyfully showed me the caption: "Sub Apnay *und Miss Naheed Kay Paas Jama Kara Dain". The 'Fay' was chopped and had become a 'Laam'. "Yaar Fakhri Bhai, Miss Naheed Tay Pareshan Ho Jayen Gi? Hain Ji?" I cursed the damn calibration! I told Mr. Javed that we can't change the font as it would be different than the rest of the page. He took his pen and made it 'Fay' – "Jadoon Chal Si Tay Don't Worry!"

By 3:00 AM, the newspaper had started taking shape. Javed Sahib gave me an advertisement to develop for a calling cab service. The owner was a guy named Raja Basharat. Javed Sahib told me to put "24 Ghantay Khuli…Har Waqt Tayyar…Aap Ki Company", in a jumbo size font. I told him that there will still be space left as the advertisement was supposed to cover of half back page. He said, "Ohdi Picture Paa Day Yaar". He gave me a picture of a very young Raja Basharat, maybe from his college days, wearing a pinkish shirt and smiling sheepishly. Javed Sahib told me that this was maybe his first picture in his village long before he moved to New York.

I told him that this picture doesn't go with the advertisement. He yawned that it's already 4:00 in the morning and we need to hit the press by 5:00, so don't argue. He added that Raja loves to appear young and is also paying top dollars for the advertisement –

"Jadoon Chal Si Tay Don't Worry!" I completed the advertisement, checked it on the monitor, and printed it. Javed Sahib hastily pasted the advertisement on the back page together with the picture. We dashed for the press and it took us another hour before I could head home. The paper was scheduled to be at the Manhattan stores by 1:00 PM, Queens by 2:00, Brooklyn by 3:00, etc.

I came home, ate something, and slept like dead. The phone ring woke me up around 2:20. It was the editor Sahib. He told me to go to the nearest grocery store and check out the newspaper, at once. I walked to a Desi store in Corona, and found a fresh copy of the newspaper. I browsed through the newspaper feeling very happy and proud, until I got to the back page...There emerged a picture of Raja Basharat clad in pink with a virgin smile and a font 36 bold caption..."24 Ghantay Khuli...Har Waqt Tayyar...Aap Ki Kameeni", along with his mobile number. The 3rd dot of "Pay" was chopped and it had become a "Yay".

I told Javed Sahib, "Jadoon Chal Si Tay Don't Worry!" He replied that you are not familiar with Pothohari Punjabi, so you can't comprehend what Raja is telling me right now.

Anyway, Raja was a good guy after all. He settled with the newspaper by just not paying for the advertisement. Later, I learned from Javed Sahib that Raja's business actually boomed after that advertisement and he never changed his mobile number.

ASI SHAFIQULLAH NIAZI

The day was Jan. 10th, 1989. We were attending a relative's marriage at Sheesh Mahal hall in North Nazimabad...

I parked our car right in front of the main entrance and the family headed in for a luscious dinner. I had just installed a new car-deck (generosity of my mother) in the car in spite of my dad's opposition. Also, I had spent Rs. 500-600 on some new cassettes. The cassettes were put in such a way that my father would not be able to spot them, as he would ride in the front seat. One Na'at cassette was visible for camouflage. Folks who know my father know the reason.

We came out of the hall around 12:30 in the night, went to the parking spot and "Phir Uskay Baad Chiraghon Main Roshni Naa Rahi". All the lights of Sheesh Mahal Hall started to look dim and the Hyderabadi dishes seemed to be coming back the wrong way. The car was gone!! Some people stopped to sympathize and we stopped some from mocking. We were told to lodge a report ASAP as the car right now could be taking part in "Waardaat". My father and I took a cab to the North Police Station and the rest of the family went home.

Sri Lankan Dessert

A constable greeted us with a pathetic look and informed that ASI Sahib will lodge the report. It was around 1:00 AM when we entered the room where he could be found.

The ASI was unconscious in his chair with his head turned towards the entrance. Isa Khailwi's song was blaring on a nearby cassette player: "Mera Janaza Nikla, Meri Baraat Ban Kar!" with his gun lying on the table, pointing towards his fat belly. The ASI was snoring loud with one hand on the gun and one on the phone. The snoring was causing a disturbance to two other guys who were trying to sleep squatting on the floor. They must have been bad elements apprehended by the officer himself. Their Izaar-Bands were knotted together and then to the leg of ASI's desk.

I dared not wake him up. My father feared that a phone ring or a louder snore might end the career of a decorated police officer. The constable accompanying us woke him up.

"Niazi Sahib, Report Aee Hai!"

His lumpy body shook with a tremor and then, without looking up, he tried to act as if he's been thinking about a difficult case like Liaquat Ali's murder. He slowly put his index finger in the trigger cage of the gun and started revolving the gun between us and him. His red eyes focused on Neeli's picture thoughtfully, showing from underneath the glass-top of his desk. He unseeingly kicked the squatting fellows to make sure they are still there.

He then looked up.

"Thaana Naarth Janab, ASI Saifullah Niazi on duty", and tried to touch his name tag but pointed to the wrong side of his chest. With the other hand, he turned-off the cassette player.

"Gaari Ki Chori Ki Report Likhani Hai!"

"Kaunsi Gaari?" He tried to bring some authority into his voice.
"Ji Who Jo Hamari Chori Ho Gayee Hai!"

"Yeh Aap Ka Kaun Hai?" He asked my father pointing at me.
"Yeh Mera Beta Hai!"

"Accha! Yeh Tumharay Kaun Hain?" He asked me.
"Yeh Meray Walid Hain".

He explained that it's his duty not to overlook any details while writing the report and then rolled-up his sleeves. He pulled a register out of the drawer and got a hold of the Piano ball pen which was hanging with a string.

"Gaari Ka Malik Kaun Hai? Koi Saa Naam Bataden". We replied and he started writing down.

"Gaari Ki Nummer Plate Ka Nummer?"
"219 532"

"Gaari Ka Color?"
"White!"

"Yaani Chittaa?"
"Ji!"

Then he revealed his brownish-orange teeth studded with pure gold ones under the thick canopy of moustache.

"Chitti Garian Jaasti Uthti Hain! Hamara to Raat Din Kam Yeh Hi Hai! Abbay Noo Aaakh Chitti Gaari Na Khareeday!"
"OK!"

"Hor Kinni Garian Hain Gi Tuaday Kol Munday?"

Sri Lankan Dessert

"Ji Bas Aik hi Hai!"

"Aur Who Hi Chori Ho Gayee?"

At this time, he sank in the seat a little more and started giggling. His red eyes were half-closed and plump shoulders bounced up and down and his jelly-belly bounced to and fro. The sound of his laughter was like dragging a heavy wooden box on some mosaic floor.

He then reached for his bulging front pocket and tried to get the cigarette box out. The box got stuck because of too much stuff in there. He had to first take out the pink comb, a round mirror with Marlin Monroe's famous pose, a half used Paan, few rubber bands, safety pins and an open tube of Araldite. He put back the stuff and opened the Red&White packet.

The "investigation" got suspended during all this time and was further delayed because of not finding a matchbox. Then, he rang a bell on his desk and a constable brought him the matchbox. He told the constable to put it back in the squatting fellows pocket as it was found during his Tafteesh.

Then, he gazed at my father with one eye almost closed and the eyebrow raised. Now that's a killer as it's usually the other eyebrow that the cops raise.

"Gaari Ka Model?"
"Toyota Corolla, 82"

"Lo, Is Nay To Chori Hona Hi Tha!"
"Gaari Aap Start Chore Kay To Shadi Main Nahin Chalay Gaye Thay?"
"Ji Nahin".

"Humm, Kadi Lock Gaari Chori Ho Jaye To Is Ka Matbal Hay Kay Chore Kamiyaab Ho Gaya Hai!"
"Ji?"

"Aap Ko Kaisay Pata Laga Kay Gaari Chori Ho Gayee Hai?"
"Ji Gaari Jahan Park Ki Thee, Wahan Mojaud Nahin Hai. Aisay Pata Chala Kay Gaari Chori Ho Gaye Hai."

He stared at me.

"Tum Kiya Kartay Ho?"
"Ji Main Student Hoon!"

"Oye Student Tay Ho, Par Kartay Kiya Rahtay Ho?"
"Ji Main To Harwaqt Parhaai Karta Rahta Hoon".

"Kahan Par Parhtay Ho?"
"Main N.E.D. Main Parhta Hoon"

"Accha! Meray Vi Aik Rashtaydar N.E.D Kaalij Main Hain!"
"Ji Accha! Who Kiya Parhatay Hain?"

"O Na! Wo Constable Hain, Wahan Duty Detay Hain!"
"Ji".

"Report Tayyar Hai. Kacchi Waali Banaai Hai Takay Gaari Jald Mil Jai. Pakki Lakhao to Adalat Say Milaygee".
"Inspector Sahib, Gaari Mil To Jaye Gee?"

"Milnay Ko To Suboh Vi Mil Sakdi Hai. Warna To Us Nay Ab Tak Quettay Pahunch Jaana Hai!"
"Inspector Sahib, 2-3 Ghanton Main Quetta Kaisay Jaa Sakti Hai? Aap Please Radio Control Pay Inform To Karden!"

He looked discomforted. "Aap Ko Chorion Ka Hum Say Ziayada Pata

Hai? Apna Nummer Chhad Jayen, Pata Lagay Tay Fir Phone Kar Dayen Gay!"

We left Thaana Naarth. The next day, we got a call from Gulberg P.S. that our car was found at an "undisclosed" location. The police had towed it to the Police Station. We went to the Gulberg P.S., found the car minus the deck with a broken ignition key-switch. We paid Rs. 2,000 for Mithai to the jubilant staff and brought the car home.

Well, the car was back but my Pioneer deck worth Rs. 1,600 was missing. That was a big amount in the N.E.D. days. My favorite cassettes were gone too. We had the car back but never dared to put a stereo in it again.

ASIAN WHATEVER

These ideas will help generate great revenues for the Pakistani government and help our dear country become the once promised: "Asian Tiger/Cat/Mouse/Reptile/Whatever/At least something!"

Sadaqah:

There would be Sadaqah boxes installed in front of every home, business, and market. To survive the next 24 hours without being killed, abducted, arrested, getting wounded, being handed over to FIA, FIT, IB, ISI, and CIA/FBI, etc., there would be Sadaqah put in the collectors for the government. This follows the Islamic spirit as Sadaqa evades evil.

Shukrana:

There would be Shukrana collection centers in each street of every town. Shukrana would be necessary for each 24 hours passed without sniper killings, bomb blasts, children not falling in manholes, a bus loaded with passengers not turning turtle, people standing on a sidewalk not being crushed by the bus loaded with passengers turning turtle, live wires not falling on people, dogs not biting the people who are running from the live wires falling on people. If your Shukrana box is empty, make sure your Sadaqah box is full.

Jaan Ki Amaan:

A special revenue collection for Karachi. This would be paid to the people who ask for it. This would make sure that car liftings don't turn into corpse liftings because of uncooperative public. All robberies would be insured for life (life only) and all ransoms paid would get the kidnapped person back. Don't confuse Jaan Ki Amaan with Bhatta. Bhatta was in the old days of political parties; Jaan Ki Amaan is in the new "real" democracy.

Imaan kI Amaan:

A very handy revenue if religious political parties ever come into power. The collection would be done after every prayer and twice in the Friday prayers. This would ensure that one is still part of the majority religion, whatever it is.

Nichhawar:

This will be performed when any of the beautiful and smart VIPs would come out of their VIP comforts into the city to block the traffic. The thousands of people stranded on the sidewalks, if there are any sidewalks, would Nichhawar currency notes on their leaders. Also, "Chashm-e-Baddoor" will be chanted during a Nichhawar.

Bukhul Tax:

Bukhul, or misery, has been condemned in Islam since day one. The people seemed to be practicing Bukhul by blaming price hikes. They tend to eat a single bread instead of two because the bread is too expensive. This practice is against national interests. Some people are worse as they eat once in three days. All these people are causing a great loss to the local and global economy. So, whenever there is a price increase in edibles, the government would be asking for Bukhul Tax. An even better idea is to deduct this amount from the salary every time the prices go up.

Imaam Zaamin:

Whenever a VIP travels abroad for greater benefits to the poor masses, he is putting his life at risk. He is traveling with his family, friends, and servants together with other VIPs and their families...to Singapore on his way to Paris. For whom? For the thankless public. If something happens on this trip, Maaz-Allah, Pakistan would be without so many VIPs. So before every VIP journey, there would be Imaam Zaamin contribution by the people, for the people, to the VIP.

Harjaana:

This will be imposed on people who try to defame the government. For example, a man commits suicide because of constant hunger and joblessness. He is defaming the government instead of cursing his own screwed-up "Muqaddar". A rape victim in a village jumps into a canal, that's her fault. First of all, there is no water in the canal... so she lands on hard surface. Again, she did not try to stay alive until she could be taken to the hospital 200 miles away and given expired injections.

All these people defame the country, which means the government, which means the VIPs. Hence a "Khudkushi" Harjaana will be imposed on all families who have someone dead without the government's direct involvement. A list will be made of each family every week, and if someone is missing from the list, Harjaana has to be paid.

Kuffaara:

This used to be called "Muk-Muka", but that gives an impression of some wrong-doing. Kuffaara, on the other hand, purifies people from their sins and raises the foreign exchange levels as well. If someone has killed a fellow Pakistani, snatched the money from another Pakistani, and/or usurped the land of a third Pakistani, he can confess to the authorities, pay Kuffara in person, and be free from all of his sins until next time. It would be advisable to tell the authorities beforehand so that Kuffaara could be paid in advance.

Hadiya:

This is not the old "Rishwat" system where the giver and taker go to Hell. No way! In Hadiya, both parties go to Heaven. There will be a set Hadiya for each type of job that needs to be done. Hadiya mixed with "Nazraana" will take the ordinary man to the next level in Heaven where he has direct intimation with the higher-ups. Giving Hadiya to the government elite and "Bakhshish" to the not so elite will make rivers of milk and honey flow through our country.

BADI MUSHKIL HAI

Inspired by a song from a Hindi movie:

Hum Bhi Superpower Hotay, Hamaray Jahaz Raaj Kartay!

Jahan Jispar Chahtay, Hum Foran Hi Waar Kartay!

Haan Mujahid Hay, Shaheed Hay, Ghazi Hay, Fighter Hay...Designer Nahin...

Badi Mushkil Hay...

Haan Mujahid Hay, Shaheed Hay, Ghazi Hay, Fighter Hay...Designer Nahin...

Badi Mushkil Hay...

Ji Karta Hay Time Machine Banaon, Aur 500 Saal Peechay Jaaoon!

Aur Wahan Jaa Kar Saari Inventions, Muslims Kay Naam Karaaoon!

Haan Plumber Hay, Painter Hay, Tailor Hay, Welder Hay...Inventor Nahin...

Sri Lankan Dessert

Badi Mushkil Hay...

Haan Plumber Hay, Painter Hay, Tailor Hay, Welder Hay...Inventor Nahin...

Badi Mushkil Hay...

Hum Bhi Shaan Say Chaltay, Aur Na Yun Khuwaar Hotay!

Green Passport Ki Jhalak Dikha Kar, Immigration Say Paar Hotay!

Haan Artist Hay, Dentist Hay, Leftist Hay, Rightist Hay ...Scientist Nahin...

Badi Mushkil Hay...

Haan Artist Hay, Dentist Hay, Leftist Hay, Rightist Hay ...Scientist Nahin...

Badi Mushkil Hay...

Fiza Ho Ya Khala Ho, Hamaray Sar Pay Taaj Hota!

Samandaron Ki Tah Main, Apna Hi Raaj Hota!

Haan Teacher Hay, Student Hay, Tutor Hay, Master Hay...Researcher Nahin...

Badi Mushkil Hay...

Haan Teacher Hay, Student Hay, Tutor Hay, Master Hay...Researcher Nahin...

Badi Mushkil Hay...

Fakhri

Goray Kaalay Sab Aatay, Aur Apni Faryaden Laatay!

Hamari Imdaad Pay Chaltay, Aur Hamara Diya Khaatay!

Haan Actor Hay, Player Hay, Singer Hay, Dancer Hay...Engineer Nahin...

Badi Mushkil Hay...

Haan Actor Hay, Player Hay, Singer Hay, Dancer Hay...Engineer Nahin...

Badi Mushkil Hay...

Worldbank Ko Loan Detay, IMF Ko Kaan Pakarwaatay!

America, Russia, Germany, Japan, Hamaara Udhaar Khaatay!

Haan Tulla Hay, Mulla Hay, Aalim Hay, Naazim Hay...Technologist Nahin...

Badi Mushkil Hay...

Haan Tulla Hay, Mulla Hay, Aalim Hay, Naazim Hay...Technologist Nahin...

Badi Mushkil Hay...

BUSHARRAF'S CAMPAIGN SPEECH

My idea of a Presidential Campaign Speech from former Pakistani President Perdase Busharraf:

Meray Zaleel Hamwatno, after looking at the past and present presidents, I have (Mulk-o-Qaum Kay Bahtar Mafad Main) made-up my mind to become the president of Pakistan again. I don't need your vote or your pathetic support. All I need is a "deal" to deal with my presidency.

What motivates me for this position is that this is the only job in Pakistan that does not require any education, experience, qualification, integrity, character, political background, statesmanship, or public support. All I need is "Foran" Support from a Master White country and "Majbooran" Support from a Brother Brown country.

It's not that I don't have any qualifications to become the president of Pakistan...I do have a foreign passport, assets outside of the country, and my kids speak English. I prostrate when I see a white guy and spit when I see a Pakistani. All I am looking for now is any kind of MRO (Mauj-Manatay Raho Ordinance). Moreover, this is the only job in the world that when you decide to step down (and step out of the country), you bear no responsibility whatsoever. This is the yummiest part!

I have made-up my manifesto which is comprised of promises and more promises. Most of these will be fulfilled as they will be part of the deal. The rest of them are not even worth mentioning so why bother fulfilling. Check out for yourself....

- Milk will be sold for Rs. 5,000 per 10ml, Sugar will be Rs. 20,000 for 10g and buying flour will be illegal. This will help maintain the economy according to IMF guidelines.

- The Indus and Jhelum rivers will be sold to our innocent neighboring country as a token of apology because we invaded them twice. The proceeds will silently be proceeded to my bank account. I don't like to announce my good deeds.

- Electricity consumers will be electrocuted. We can't have our industry compete with any other country. Competition is aggression and Islam is a religion of peace and sacrifice, etc. etc.

- The Pakistani army will be rented out to the highest bidder. I already have generous offers from our only trusted friend across the Atlantic. They may outsource it to the only source of peace in the Middle East which is surrounded by a dozen terrorist countries. Anyway, politics is not my subject. This time the proceeds will be divided between me and the top brass...Saday Naal Raho Gay Tay Aish Karo Gay!!

- Since GHQ will be deserted now, I will help move the army headquarters of the only good country in the world to Chaklala. This will stem-out so many rumors and help us promote the War on Error.
- All Pakistan born will require a visa to enter or leave Pakistan and will need to register their visits at the Brown Water

Company. This should not be of any concern at all as Pakistanis have consumed brown water, dark brown water, and even "black water" all their lives. Only the following people will not require a Pakistani visa:
- Any white guy
- A Sheikh Sahib coming to kill wildlife in Pakistan
- Any soldier wearing uniform other than Pakistan army
- IMF/World Bank officials who come to check my progress

➢ Sabhon Ko Pata Hona Chahiye, we will break all the Kashkols and replace them with bigger buckets. I have already handed the contract of bigger buckets to my acquaintance with 50% commission. We will setup "Sasta Kashkol Bazaar" where each Zaleel Awam will be given a bucket big enough to beg from the entire world.

➢ As the "silenced" majority is with me, I already know that I have One, yaani kay Won. All the votes that will be casted in as "Yes" will be considered as "Yes". All the votes casted in as "No" will be considered as "No Way". And as the silenced majority is with me, all the votes not casted will be considered "Considered". Remember, my "Atrandom" held in 2002? Whoever claimed that I lost the "Atrandom", was lost at random.

➢ Whoever criticizes or makes fun of my moderately democratic progressive enlightened ultra liberated government, will be picked up from his/her house, never to be seen again. We have established an export persecution bureau where all such fundamental extremists will be exported out of the country. The proceeds will be used to buy an island. I like islands in the Mediterranean while Begum Sahiba likes more of a tropical touch!!

➢ I am liked so much in the army and outside of Pakistan and inside of Afghanistan, that the US president named his dog after me. You have seen what Me and Myself have given to the country. Still, I want to turn this country 360 degrees around. This turn around reminds me of our Afghan policy which about turned and turned around. You all know how much wealth was looted and plundered while the political parties were in power; now it's my turn.

- Meray Zaleel Hamwatno, lets take a look at history. When Pakistan was made, we had lots of Pakistan. And the military budget was less. Now, we have lots of military with budget but less Pakistan. Why? Because of Fundamentalism. And religious extremism and terrorist exorcism. I want to change this and that. I am not Ayub Khan, Zia Ul-Haq, or Yahya; I am Mrs. Busharraf's husband.

- Coming to the topic of lawlessness, price hikes, education, feudalism...blaakh blaakh...these topics are so ugly to discuss that I am about to throw-up!

Main Zindabad
Afwaaj-e-Pakistan Paeendabad.
Asl-e-Pakistan Islamabad.

CHIEF JUSTICE BAHAAL HO GAYE HAIN

Even though it's a little late now, but we can still relate to it:

Chief Justice Bahaal Ho Gaye Hain...
Awam Behaal Ho Gaye Hain...
Nawaz Shareef Nihaal Ho Gaye Hain...
Zardari MalaMaal Ho Gaye Hain..
Chief Justice Bahaal Ho Gaye Hain...

Log Kangaal Ho Gaye Hain..
Ministers Khooshhaal Ho Gaye Hain...
Paani Bijli Khuwab-o-Khayaal Ho Gaye Hain...
Institutions Roo Ba Zawaal Ho Gaye Hain...
Chief Justice Bahaal Ho Gaye Hain...

Dhamakay Aik Wabaal Ho Gaye Hain...
Police Walay Janjaal Ho Gaye Hain...
Criminals Ziayada Fa'aal Ho Gaye Hain...
Corrupt Zarb-ul-Misaal Ho Gaye Hain..
Chief Justice Bahaal Ho Gaye Hain...

Nayaab Aata, Chawal Daal Ho Gaye Hain...
Ghareeb Bhook Say Nidhaal Ho Gaye Hain...
Insaani Huqooq Pamaal Ho Gaye Hain...
Achay Din Mahaal Ho Gaye Hain...
Chief Justice Bahaal Ho Gaye Hain...

Drone Hamlay Ziyada Filhaal Ho Gaye Hain...
Corruption Kai Qissay Lazawaal Ho Gaye Hain...
Pakistan Banay 60 Saal Ho Gaye Hain...
Naraaz Rabb-e-ZulJalaal Ho Gaye Hain...
Chief Justice Bahaal Ho Gaye Hain...

CHOROO BUDDHAY

Trying to classify "Hamaaray Baray"...If someone takes it personally, I'll take it as a compliment.

CHOROO BUDDHAY:

The usual kind...the most common species of Buzurg around. Since no one was around when they were around, it gives them the liberty to stretch it beyond seams.

"Mian Hamaray Zamanay Main To Desi Ghee Say Jharoo Di Jaati Thi..."

"Aman Jab Main Bhutto Say Milnay Multan Jail Ki Taraf Ko Gaya!"

"Uncle Bhutto Pindi Main Band Tha!"

"Abay To Band Hi Tha Na!...Bahar to Nahin Tha!...To Bhutto Nay Minjay Bola...Hakeem-Ud-Deen!!...Agar Teri Baat Maan Leta...To Aaj Hiyaan Is Haal Main Na Hota!"

TAROO BUDDHAY:

Apnay Zamanay Kay Taarzan...We are novices in this field when compared to our "Islaaf Kay Karnaamay". The other day, I was in the mall with my wife when a "Baray Mian" ran into me. Actually, he was trying to run into my wife; I barely managed to cut in the middle. "Kiya Haal Chaal Hain Mian!" he inquired while staring at the my Biwi. Then, as a gesture of "Shafqat" he put a hand on her head which I had to remove after a struggle. "Kiya Shopping Ka Irada Hay?"..."Ji Ab Nahin Hay". I replied and we made an emergency exit.

These Taarzans were the ones that used to stand near college girls' van stops. As soon as the van would come to a halt, the Buzurgwar will start muttering an "Aaa Aaa Aaa Aaa Aaa" with a hanging lower lip. People would think that he is trying to woo the chicken in the alley while the seasoned spectator is trying to woo the chick who just stepped out.

AAJIZ BUDDHAY:

If you think depression is not contagious, think again! With a deep cynical look, they will transport this doomsday news to you. "No doctor can answer this question...Kay Meri 3 Bajay Waali Gas 5 Bajay Kiyon Aati Hay?"

They just have too much mileage in all the wrong areas. Suppose you coughed in their vicinity..."Lo! Har-Taraf To Jaraseem Phela Diyay, Ab Kiya Faida". The next sentence would be "Mian Jab Main Aap Ki Umar Ka Tha! Majaal Hay Kabhi Khaansi Waansi Aajay".

If, "Khudanakhuwasta", you start a conversation on politics, this is usually the first line: "Abay Is Ki To $#@$%^&...Yeh Kiya Kar Lay Ga! Main To Is Kay Baap Ko Bhi Jaanta Hoon 1920 Say..."

CUSTOM BUDDHAY:

These are the self appointed ombudsmen. They have the right to question anything about you and then check it out for themselves in case you are hiding something. OK, so you are grocery shopping and your bad luck – a custom Buddha spots you.

This is usually how the conversation starts: "Sahih Sahih Bataao! How much do you computer guys actually make?" First he X-rays you to see if you are telling the truth. Then he customs your shopping cart with his hand already in it. "Acha! Yeh $3.99 Wali cheez lee hay! Do Kiyon Lay Leen?" The third sentence would be: "My grandson has just completed high school and is trying to kill boring weekends. You should tutor him about "Computer Shomputer" and help him get an 80K job."

HITLER BUDDHAY:

The last to show up on Fridays and then try to get into the 1st Saff. Any youngster sitting in the 1st Saff is like a quail spotted by Farooq Leghari. Just the other day, this Madd-e-Zillahu dashed from the washroom (forgetting to flush) and beat the whole Masjid (literally) to paratroop just in front of the Imam in the middle of the sermon.

Imam Sahib, a little shaken, carried on. After glancing victoriously at the helpless crowd, Hazrat started paying close attention to...himself. I guess sneezing, coughing, clearing throat, hiccups, burping, and gargling right next to the mic is considered part of Taqwa.

This is what the sinners could hear from a distance..."Jo Yeh Baat Maan Lay Ga Woh Inshallah 'Bhaaaar' Main Jaye Ga!...Aur Jo Yeh Baat Nahin Maanay Ga Who 'Bhaaaaar' Main Jaye Ga!...Jab Banda Fajar Main Uthta Hay To Sab Say Pahlay 'Urghhhhhhh' Mahsoos Karta Hay...Aik To Insaan Gunah Karay, Us Kay Baad 'Ahaaa Ahaaa' Bhi Karay?...Is Say Bahtar Hay Kay Tanhai Main Beth Kar 'Shuroon Shuroon Hichik Shuroon' Kar Lay."

EXOTIC DISHES

These are some of the ever popular exotic Pakistani dishes that have been popular for ages. They can be enjoyed all year long and are guaranteed to keep you coming back for more.

Awami Kaleja:

This is an old traditional dish loved by everyone. It's cheap to prepare and nowadays readily available. In fact, this is one of the dishes that costs nothing to the government.

Ingredients: Awam with Kaleja, Price Hikes, Lawlessness, Unemployment, Deegar-Masael.

Recipe: Marinate the Awam for 30-40 years in Price Hikes, Lawlessness, and Unemployment. Add power outages, water shortages, and road blocks for extra taste. The Awami Kaleja will start cooking by itself. Female Awam may be exposed to rapes and assaults for a touch of class. Add Deegar-Masael for garnishing. Awami Kaleja gives guaranteed results when cooked on Rs. 100 per Litre gasoline.

Murgh-e-Musallah:

Mashallah, this is the fastest prepared dish in our history and is ready in no time. It only costs as much as one would spend in getting Musallah.

Ingredients: Someone Musallah, Someone with a Murgha.

Recipe: Just bring someone with a Murgha close to someone who is Musallah. Before you know it, the Murgha will change hands and that's it. If the one with the Murgha tries to somehow delay the preparation of the dish, he/she will be turned into Bakra Dum-Pukht.

TeriMaaki Soup:

Don't confuse this with the Oriental Teriyaki thing. This is a pure Desi outdoor dish. The ideal time for this dish is a hot summer afternoon.

Ingredients: Cattle, Hot Weather, Traffic Jams, Long Queues.

Recipe: Just have the cattle stand for 2-3 hours anywhere in the scorching sun for seasoning. Ideal times for this soup are traffic jams at VIP movements, the last day to pay bills in front of banks, cattle stranded at transport strikes, etc. The dish is at its peak when an ingredient reaches the bank window in the heat of the day to pay the bill and is told that timings are over. It's a common practice to yell the name of the dish repeatedly once the soup starts coming out.

Shahi Qorma:

This is a dish just made for the Royals. The public has no access to it. Once someone starts tasting it, it's impossible to let go.

Ingredients: Public Leaders, Public Money, More Public Money.

Recipe: This dish is prepared usually by the Chief of Chef Staff. Mix public leaders thoroughly with public money and leave standing for some time. Keep on adding public money as it keeps on disappearing in the Qorma. After sometime, there has to be a shake-up in the dish. The Chief of Chef Staff takes some leaders out and put some other leaders in. Then, he adds lots of public money into the Qorma again. Occasionally, the team of Chefs also starts tasting the Qorma to make sure its up to Royal standards.

VIP Broast:

This is a long awaited dish that is the public's fantasy. It's just that no one is coming forward to prepare it. If Inshallah, one or two people start preparing it, soon this dish will become the norm of the day. All this dish requires is a bunch of VIPs and a big pot of burning oil.

Ingredients: VIPs (as many as possible), salt and red pepper, lots of oil.

Recipe: Undress the VIPs and put salt and pepper in all the openings. When you think there's no room left to insert anymore, shake the VIP and add some more. Leave the VIP screaming for about 2-3 hours, for best results. Now pour the oil in a big container and preheat as long as you like. When the oil starts boiling like crazy, start putting VIPs in one after the other. The VIP flesh usually produces a bad smell, so be sure to cover up your nose. When the VIP fat starts coming out in the oil, the Broast is ready. Can serve up to 180 Million.

FASAAD FI SABILILLAH

Here are few "concerns" about any Maulvi Sahib giving the Khutba and leading the Friday prayers in any mosque in the world:

- Will the Imam Sahib be wearing Shalwar-Kameez or a "Western Dress"? What is the guarantee of the Namaz being valid in a "Western dress"? How long has the Maulana been leading prayers in a "Western Dress"?

- How long is the Imam's beard? Is it equal to or more than "One Musht"? Can we measure it everytime before the Namaz?

- Is the Sheikh a Wahabi, Salafi, Muqallid, Ghair-Muqallid, Ahle-Hadeeth, or Asnaa Ashri?

- If a Muqallid, is he Hanafi, Sha'fi, Maliki or Hanbli?

- If Hanafi, is he from the Deobandi school of thought or Barelvi?

- If Barelvi, which Silsila is he from? Qadri? Naqshbandi? Chisti? Nizaami? Suharwardi?

- Braazer, Blease Abboint an Arab Imam as the Arabs Simbly Bray Better!

- Oh Ji…Eh Imam Jehra Hay Karachi Da Hay Ga! Tussan Ainj Karo Jay Lahore Da Imam Aithay Start Kar Chado…Hain Ji!

- Lahore Kay Imam Kay Peechay Namaz Late Khabool Hoti Hay…Hyderabadi Imams have quick Khabooliat.

- How many Surahs does the Imam know by heart besides Surah Kauthar?

- What Tajweed school does he follow: Hifs? Warsh? What do you mean, "What is Tajweed"?

- When was the last time the Imam comsumed "Jhatka chicken"? Eating one bite of Jhatka violates 40 years of Namaz!

- Does the Sheikh "enjoy" music and movies? I have heard from someone somewhere that if the Imam has listened to music in the past year, the whole neighborhood will get the punishment!

- How long are the Imam's trousers? Does he fold them? If yes…why? If not…why?

- What does the Imam do in his spare time? Was he ever found in "Aisi Waisi" places? Did he do a "Mukammal Istighfar" after going to (Ma'az Allah) "Aisi Waisi" places?

FUDGET

This is the Annual Pakistani Budget Speech and can be used again and again as needed:

My dear Higher-ups in Washington and oh dear Bottoms-up in Pakistan, this is your Finance Sinister presenting the 2012 Fudget.

As you know the economy would not Budge an inch. We wanted to "Budge-it", so we prepared a "Budget". The economy still would not Budge. So, the Cheap Executive told me to "Fudge-it" like IT professionals fudge data. So again this is the Finance Sinister with the "2012 Fudget speech".

This Fudget will make Pakistan comparable to Japan (in size) and will make the Ethiopian economy envy us. This fudget is according to the aspirations of the government and VIPs. We promise that there will be no Mini-Fudgets except maybe a dozen or two.

Now lets take a look at some of the Haay-Haay-Lites:

➤ The National Fudget has a volume of 842 Billion. This Volume will put Pressure on the Masses and raise their temperature. I would like to tell you that I have studied Physics from University of TantaRama at UltaLayria.

- 200 Billion have been set aside for debt retirement. 50 Billion have been set aside for my own retirement.

- The high-end commercial financial business overdraft has been curtailed by –0.3% of collateral asset mark-up evaluation for ad-hoc bank clean T/Ts encompassing the capital gains overflow trade trend. Whoever has included this in the speech should see me afterwards.

- 100 Billion have been reserved for the Defense Staff. "200 Bullions" have been reserved for the wives of the Defense Staff.

- My poor Pakistanis, what's wrong with you....At a time when the Cheap Executive has bright ideas of breaking the country...all you think about is breaking the bread? You have to grow-up...I mean grow-up your own bread.

- The previous finance sinisters, "Surcharge Aziz", "Shan-o-Shaukat Aziz" etc. levied so many taxes on poor people. Actually people always means poor. So, as I was saying, there were so many Sur-Charges forced on people; our government replaced all of them by "Sir-Charges". The "Sir" is sitting in the President's House and the "Charges" are "Charging".

- According to a health study, Oil and Ghee are bad for health. That's why we have increased the price of shortenings by Rs. 50. This will encourage the public to start eating healthy by boiling their food. Of-course we have raised the cost of Sui-Gas by 50% because another study shows that eating raw food preserves all the nutrients. In-fact, we have raised the prices of all edibles by 100% because another study shows that eating is the cause of all ailments. This will encourage the masses to drink water and eat air. Verily, 50% of the population doesn't have water and the other 50% don't have clean air and so this will encourage Pakistanis to....Let me get back to my speech.

- 90 Billion have been allocated for the domestic loans servicing. 89 Billion have been allocated for the Presidential limousine service. The Cheap Executive told me personally that as a great service to the common man we should reduce the tariff on imported cars. So, we came-up with a formula – the bigger the engine, the smaller the duty. For example: A very uncommon man with a 0 CC engine (Paidal!) will pay 200% duty. A not so common man owning a luxury car with a 2500 CC engine, will pay 100% duty. A very common man with a Mercedes S500 with 5000 CC engine, will pay 0% duty. And, if one can import a luxury liner with a 500,000 CC engine, government will pay him from it's own pocket.

- The Tauheen-e-Risalat law was causing problems in the Capital...I mean Capitol Hill. So, we have decided to replace it with "Tauheen-e-Washington" law. This law has two corollaries:
1) Tauheen-e-World Tank
2) Tauheen-e-International Monetary Fraud
Hence, anyone who criticizes Washington or revolts against the World-Tank/IMF policies will have to pay a steep price. The steep price will be deposited in the National Exchequer.

- Our Foran Exchange policy is unaltered. If you have Black money in Rupees, Foran Exchange it into Dollars. If you have Black money in dollars, Foran Exchange into Gray money. Gray reminds me of the hair color of the President; Gray is such a beautiful color as my suit is also Gray.

- Phone charges are up by 15% and Phony charges by 20%, Milk is up by 25% and Silk is up 30%, Atta is up by 35% and Ghata is up by 40%, Income tax is up by 45% and Outcome tax by 50%.

- All subsidies have been taken back to make sure that the public can stand on its own feet and stop relying on government support. And also, to prove that what the government gives, it can take back; what people give, they can't.

- At last, there is some good news. US economy is improving which gives me the hope of getting a job in the States after I am done with Pakistan.

- I have to leave now, as I am about to attend a wedding where 10,000 people will feast on public money.

World Bank Paeend-a-Baad
Pakistan Aaeend-a-Baad

GHABAN KA CHAKKA LAGA

Inspired by the cricket world cup 2011 song:

Nas Nas Main Rag Rag Main Dollar Sa Bolay Haan Bolay!
Dharkan Ki Rag Rag Main Corruption Si Koonday!

Nas Nas Main Rag Rag Main Dollar Sa Bolay Haan Bolay!
Dharkan Ki Rag Rag Main Corruption Si Koonday!

Imaandariyon Ko Dher Kar!
Imaandariyon Ko Dher Kar!
Mil Kay Zara Tu Her-Pher Kar!

Agay Barh Kay Aur Dat Kay Ab Tu Ghaban Ka Chaka Laga!

Ghaban Ka Chaka Laga Re Jag Main...Ghaban Ka Chaka Laga!
Ghaban Ka Chaka Laga Re Jag Main...Ghaban Ka Chaka Laga!

Shor-o-Ghul Ho Halchal Lagay Ronay Sari Public Phir Se!
Note Hon Karraray, Lagay Haraam Ki Baazi Ab Phir Se!

Shor-o-Ghul Ho Halchal, Lagay Ronay Sari Public Phir Se!
Note Hon Karraray, Lagay Haraam Ki Baazi Ab Phir Se!

Duniya Say Tu Maal Chupa!
Duniya Say Tu Maal Chupa!
Din Raat Bas Tu Maal Bana!

Agay Barh Kay Aur Dat Kay Ab Tu Ghaban Ka Chaka Laga!

Ghaban Ka Chaka Laga Re Jag Main...Ghaban Ka Chaka Laga!
Ghaban Ka Chaka Laga Re Jag Main...Ghaban Ka Chaka Laga!

Ghaban Ka Chaka Laga Re Jag Main...Ghaban Ka Chaka Laga!
Ghaban Ka Chaka Laga Re Jag Main...Ghaban Ka Chaka Laga!

GHAREEB NAY PAIT BHAR KAR ROTI KHALI

My perception of different reactions that would follow a news like this.

President

People voted for our party for Roti, Kapra and Makan...not for Roti and "Saalan". Looks like someone has eaten Saalan with Roti...this is a conspiracy against democracy and an effort to tarnish the image of our government. The Media should to be careful to not to spread anti-democratic stuff like this. The BB Shaheed's mission will continue...We will complete 50 years...I am going to Dubai to check my accounts...Pakistan Khao Piyo...Yaani Khapay!

Prime Minister:

We are sad that we just lost a dedicated party worker. Establishment is behind such dirty tactics, but I call upon all the political parties to come forward and draft a resolution to curb such incidents in the future.

Leader of Opposition:

We had made it possible to buy a Roti for two rupees. But you need to eat 16 such Rotis to fill your stomach. If the poor are allowed to eat as many Rotis as they can, how can they value the worth of a single Roti? Who will vote for us next time? Is this the work of agencies?

Maulana:

According to Islam, eating is Haraam...(a big burp!!)...unless someone is a Maulvi...(another burp!). So, either this person is an absolute Kaafir and should be killed or he is a Maulvi...but then this is not even news in the latter case.

Federal Food Minister:

Again, this speaks volumes for our government. Not only was a person allowed to be near a Roti, but he actually consumed it. This was not possible in the days of dictatorship and we have to praise our government and democracy for it.

Administration:

We are still looking into how a flour bag made its way to the public. We assure you that the people responsible for this will not go unpunished.

India:

Kaljog Hay Maharaaj! Looks like this person is a cousin of Ajmal Kassab – Akmal Naanbai. We want the ISI chief to report to the Chandni Chowk police station and explain this in full details. If people start eating with their bellies full in Pakistan, then they would turn their attention towards other problems like...India.

Foreign Powers:

This is bad news for the war on error...I mean the war on terror. In our opinion, this person is getting ready to plot an attack on our vital interests. That's the only reason that he stored food in his body which could be used later to spread extremism. We are trying to locate him with our satellite and once we get his GPS coordinates...!!

Ghareeb Aadmi:

Ya Allah Shukar Hay Tu Nay Pait Bhara...Ab Aglay Maheenay Sahi...

GIRGIT TEAM LINEUP

This could be the probable team lineup for the national Girgit team. This batting order can even win matches against teams like Namibia, Peru, Angola, Mali, or Papua New Guinea.

It's equally useful for the opposing side in matches against teams like Australia, England, India, and Sri Lanka...well any team that can play first class. With the democracy at the Helm of the affairs, our team will change so many colors in bright outfits that it will outclass any Girgit. Lets look at the final twelve:

1) Often Unfit
2) Often Misfit
3) Bookie
4) Rookie
5) Out of Form
6) Out of Farm
7) Qaumi Zero
8) Sifar Star
9) 10 miles per hour
10) 15 runs per career
11) No Balls
12) Yes Boss

HELLUCINATIONS

It was as hot as a summer day with load shedding...OK, not quite but close. I was at the very end of a long line formed under a sign displaying "Hisaab-Kitaab". Who knows how many people were in line, as I couldn't see the front.

Then, a couple of horrible-looking angels started coming my way. They looked at my starving being and started laughing. "He! He! He!", one said, "What a clown...He is standing in the VIP queue!" The second one was bending over with laughter, "He thinks he deserves to get Hisaab...I checked his letter-of-deeds...Totally Pathetic!" They pushed me out of the line as stronger people used to push me out of the utility stores and bill payment lines. I was perplexed and dejected as to where to go.

At that very instance, a thunderous voice declared to someone at the front of the line, "Go To Hell!" That guy was then escorted by the same laughing angels who had now wiped their eyes and were suddenly trying to act serious. I recognized that person when the three passed by me.

He was a feuda, turned politician, turned Billionaire, turned foreign national, turned Prime Minister, turned Trillionaire, turned dead. He exclaimed, "What the Hell!" The angels remarked, "Hellcome to Hell...We are big fans of you...Let's take you to the Red Zone". I decided to follow them and reached close enough to peek inside the VIP enclave!

Subhan-Allah...The Red Zone was actually the Red Hot Zone! Huge houses built inside live erupting volcanoes. They looked way bigger than my 40 sq. yds. hen-pen on Earth, I thought. Sizzling kitchens had big personal ovens with settings starting from "Inferno" to "Helly-Gully". Precious royal crowns made of thorns and flames with matching robes and flammable pajamas! A big, bright sun used as a personal sauna and a luxurious swimming pool full of recycled waste. I never even dreamed of a swimming pool all my life, but had taken baths in the city's water supply runs that looked and smelled similar.

I saw pet snakes and scorpions the size of Punjabi movie stars...All I had in life for a pet was a starving cat that deserted me one day! And, I saw giant deaf and blind servants with all kinds of hot massage accessories, eager to serve! Jealous...I asked a guard angel, who was steaming like an old car's radiator, "What do VIPs do once they get here?"... "24/7 Hella-Gulla", he boiled.

Then I saw a VVIP convoy. An escort of 70 angels had grabbed the President with his head and all four limbs and was carrying him to the edge of the hell. Boy! I sighed with envy...what a lucky chap! I had to walk on my two trembling legs to get down here and this sucker is getting a VVIP escort. I objected to this to an angel with Klingon looks and he smiled like the President used to smile while receiving foreign aid, "Once a VIP, always a VIP!" As soon as the team of angels delivered their precious cargo into the fathomless pit, I heard the echo of hell burping. "That's a hell of a burp", I exclaimed. The angel displayed his Klingon denture, "That's a hell of a guy!"

As soon as the President hit the bottom, other inmates started cursing at him and swearing loudly. Ahhh! Just like the elite parties they used to throw, I fantasized...when folks had too much booze to handle, they would curse and swear at each other...all signs of a "Hell of a time!" I was now adamant to get inside.

I demanded to see the custodian of hell - called the Baray Sahib, right then. The angels looked at me in disbelief and then gave me the usual pathetic reply, "Hell No! You cannot meet Baray Sahib directly!" I could see Baray Sahib setting-up his secretariat in the middle of the hell as he threw a "no-lift" glance at me and tried to look busy as hell.

He is a hell of an actor, I thought. I screamed at the top of my weak voice at the most horrible looking of angels. "Hell-o...I have braced bureaucratic attitudes all my life and Baray Sahib does not even come close to humans. Take my application to Baray Sahib for approval." He got mad as hell and snatched the letter-of-deeds from my right hand and headed straight for Baray Sahib.

"Hell Done!" I smiled to myself...but he came back and told me flatly that all hellotments have been finalized, my resume is ridiculous and supporting documents are missing. Also, I don't have any "Tallukaat" with the VIPs inside so, I better stay the hell away from hell. I asked if Baray Sahib would accept some good/bad/ugly deeds to change his mind and I may be able to grab a smaller plot of 40 sq. yds??

By this time, they all had lost their patience. I know...angels hate humans since the day they realized a better looking being has been created. They all picked me up and then threw me as far away from hell as one can see and a roar followed, "Get the Hell out of here!"

ILLACTIONS

The ILLACTIONS are going to be held soon and all the overseas Pakistanis have been overseen and overlooked. All we can do is just try to understand the Hole process and the Pole parameters. Check this out:

VOTE:

It's something that never goes in a Ballot Box but always comes out. In the Pakistani elections, even the dead people have been found casting votes. When the chimpanzees of democracy cast their Vote, it's just a Vote. When the champions of democracy cast their Vote, it's called a Veto. An old lady never voted in any elections. When asked why, she replied, "Don't vote...it encourages them!"

BALLOT BOX:

The more Opaque the Ballot Box, the more transparent the ILLACTIONS. They follow the famous principal, "Garbage Bin, Garbage Out". The Ballot Boxes are filled quickly and easily once the Authorities fill their Pallet Boxes. In the Presidential Atrandoms, folks are allowed to carry the Ballot Boxes with them in the buses, trains, etc. and cast their votes from the comfort of their homes.

Sri Lankan Dessert

But, ILLACTIONS are different; the Authorities provide their own Ballot Boxes, counted, closed, and concealed.

POLLS:

They are used by the opponents to harass each other like, "Oye, Teri Poll Khol Doonga!" Polls, once opened in the morning, close in the evening but, somehow, they remain open within the Polling Station. Sometimes, they still continue while the result is being announced. Don't confuse Polls with Poles. A Pole is what used to be part of the flag and has now been inserted into the public.

RETURNING OFFICER:

Always in a hurry to Return to his school job away from the Polls but he has no place to go as schools are closed during ILLACTIONS. Returning officers return each time with the hope that this would be the last one. Being a Schoolteacher in Pakistan is a point of no return and so they have many unhappy returns. As a last resort, they put black marks on voter's hands to make them feel ashamed of what they just committed and hope that voters would never return.

PRESIDING OFFICER:

The nearest Residing Officer from the Polling Station who could be found in a hurry. His duty is to check that only the Official Ballot Boxes, the ones filled and sealed by the government itself, are used in the counting and any unofficial Ballot Boxes tampered by public are discarded. On ILLACTIONS day, he needs to see your ID Card, your Original Passport, Bank Account Number, House Layout Plan, and your Parents Marriage Certificate, to make sure that you are legitimate...I mean to vote. However, on Atrandom Day, you could cast votes just by showing a bus ticket or a used Paan wrapper.

ELECTION COMISSIONER:

Officially called Cheat Illaction Commissioner, he is a guy who, supposedly, knows the outcome before the ILLACTIONS. During Polling, although sitting in his office in Islamabad, he keeps a keen eye on everything going on in the entire...GHQ. He usually has 20,000 undecided cases pending in his court before being appointed and pointed in the right direction.

DICTATOR:

There is no fun in the ILLACTIONS without a Dick-Tator in Power. Dick-Tators come in different uniform sizes and are available in package lengths of 10, 20, or 30 years. Usually, they decide their own package and start putting the dick in everything. Pakistan is fortunate that Dick-Tators already make the choices of President, Prime Minister, Opposition Leader, Chief of Army Staff, Chief Justice, and Foreign Minister, etc. and so the public can focus on the most important issue: electing the Deputy Naib Union Committee Assistant.

CANDIDATES:

Candy-dates are Poly-ticians, which means that they have poly-faces, none of which could be revealed to the general public. Candy-dates distribute lollipops among the public in ILLACTIONS and then suck for their whole term. Candy-dates are Candid to gain power and Bandit once assumed power.

OBSERVERS:

When you reach the polling station to find out that your vote has already been cast, you instantly become an Observer. We also have some Foreign Observers who threaten to Foran stop the Foreign Aid in case the Polls are rigged. Now, how can one say for sure if there is Pre-Poll, Per-Poll, Par-Poll and Post-Poll rigging? In fact, the

ILLACTIONS are so transparent that foreigners can see through them. The results have already been prepared by observing caution by a foreign government and will be announced by observing obedience by our own government.

KARACHI FLAVORS

Some of the Karachi flavors that we miss and long for...

Amrood:

My favorite when boarding the school bus to come home. 50p would have gotten you a nice juicy guava with a green outside and a ripe inside. Just sprinkle some chaat masala and enjoy. Or you could trade it with a friend for a cone of Faalsay!

Mangoes:

Put all the world's flavors in one pan and put only Mangoes in the other and which one would I pick?? You guessed right! I'll try to go for both! OK, back to mangoes...I personally won't trade mangoes for any other thing...and my favorite...Saroli. Hot summer afternoons used to feel much more appealing when you would put a mango to your mouth and the liquid heaven starts flowing into your being.

Jaman:

Who says "Kaali bhi Kabhi Haseen Hoti Hay"? They have never handled a Jaman before. It's the only non-gori thing that I would ever let seduce me! It would come into my life for just one month and I would spend the other eleven waiting for it.

Singharay:

My favorite after lunch, of course the lunch would be Mangoes. Soorat Mat Dekh...Seerat Dekh! Looks can be deceiving, etc. etc.

Imarti:

Aah! The sexiest of all sweets. Looks can kill and yes...complicated things attract me. Just sink your teeth in a swollen Imarti and forget everything else about this stupid world!

Gol-Gappay:

It's 3:00 in the afternoon and there's no electricity on this hot sultry day. You step outside to find refuge and there you see it...standing under a shaded Bargad...the Gol-Gappy cart. Rs. 5 used to get you a plate full of 8-10 Gol-Gappays. Fill one up with the Paani and as soon as you manage to fit it in your mouth...even KESC stops feeling like an enemy!

Gazak:

Yes, we had winters too. So, it's about 11 o' clock on a December night. A little too early for Karachi folks to go to sleep – that's the reason that you are not able to sleep in your Razai. And then, you hear the bell sounds – this means thrill. You dash out of the house and grab one pao Gazak and Revri from the vendor "of course you pay for it" and dash back in the Razai with your booty. OK, its still too early to sleep but at least now you have company.

Doodh Ki Thandi Bootle:

Yeah...the same old Coke or Pakola bottle, rinsed or not, yet filled with chilled milk, khoya, and dry fruits. My favorite "snack" after Iftaar. When the hot Roza has ended and the legendary Karachi breeze has started blowing, you can get intimate with this "gori cheez" in public and no one would mind!

Qeemay Ki Pâtés:

Hazar Baar Khaya Hay! Hazar Baar Ki Hawas Hay! The bakery in my neighborhood had the best in the world. Never tasted their like again. They would be made fresh and hot around 11 in the morning and I would be at the bakery at 10:59.

Malai:

Yes, that Karachi Malai...not what they sell here in the name of Nestlé or Puck cream. You would add sugar to it...but I would prefer Mitchell's marmalade or Ahmed's Mango jam. They say that heaven has better tastes...It better have this one!

Sri Lankan Dessert

KUCH NA SAMJHAY KHUDA KARAY KOI:

Koi Samajh Jay To Hamen Bhi Bata Day:

Dr. Qadeer Hamaray Sadar Hain!

Dr. Qadeer Hamaray Dar Badar Hain!

Dr. Qadeer Awam Ko Mahboob Hain!

Dr. Qadeer US Ko Matloob Hain!

Dr. Qadeer Ko Riha Karo!

Dr. Qadeer Qaid nahin hain, Lakin Filhaal Riha Nahin Ho Saktay!

Justice Iftikhar Bahaal Hon Gay!

Justice Iftikhar Be-haal Hon Gay!

Justice Iftikhar Hamaray Chief Justice Hain!

Justice Iftikhar Tumharay Chief Justice Hain!

Justice Iftikhar Ko Riha Karo!

Justice Iftikhar Qaid nahin hain, Lakin Filhaal Riha Nahin Ho Saktay!

Democracy Phal-Phool Rahi Hay!

Democracy Jhool Rahi Hay!

Democracy Mazboot Ho Gayee Hay!

Democracy Majboor Ho Gayee Hay!

Democracy Ko Riha Karo!

Democracy Qaid nahin hay, Lakin Filhaal Riha Nahin Ho Sakti!

Zardari nay 2 Billion dollar Khaay hain!

Zardari nay 2 Billion dollar Rakhwaay hain!

Zardari Ka NRO!

Zardari Ko Maro!

Zardari Ko Riha Karo! Who America ki Qaid main hain!

Zardari Qaid nahin hay, Lakin Filhaal Riha Nahin Ho Saktay!

Awaam Mayoos Ho Chukay Hain!

Awaam Manoos Ho Chukay Hain!

Awaam Sarkon Main Ajayengay!

Awaam Barhkon Main Ajayengay!

Sri Lankan Dessert

Awaam Aur Kitnay Zaleel Hon Gay!

Awaam Aur Kitnay Zaheen Hon Gay!

Awaam Ko Riha Karo!

Awaam Qaid nahin hay, Lakin Filhaal Riha Nahin Ho Saktay!

Umreeka Hamlay Bata Kay Karay!

Umreeka Hamlay Ghata Kay Karay!

Umreeka Hamlay Band Ho Jayengay!

Umreeka Hamlay Do-Chand Ho Jayengay!

Umreeka! Jawab Do!

Umreeka! Imdaad Do!

Umreeka Ko Qaid Karo!

Umreeka Qaid nahin hay, Lakin Filhaal Riha Nahin Ho Sakta!

MAHAWARAY SHAHAWARAY

A quick look at Urdu proverbs:

Baigaani Shaadi Main Abdullah Deewanay:

Of course Abdullah can't go berserk in his own wedding when he is sitting somber on the stage thinking about the aftermath. He can only go ecstatic when he sees someone else tying the knot and joining the club. Although we would recommend Abdullah not to make fun of other people's miseries.

Soot Na Kapaas, Julahay Say Latham Latha:

You don't need Soot and Kapaas when you have "Lath". How much Soot and Kapaas you'll get depends upon the size of the Lath. If you want to look democratic, then just carry some carrots with it. This strategy works! You don't believe me? Ask the Pakistani government.

Jaib Main Nahin Daanay, Mian Chalay Bhunanay:

Mians are very smart. Why carry Daanay when the Bhoonnay Waala has plenty. Just make sure to get there when the Daanay Bhoonna has started so you don't have to wait.

900 Choohay Kha Kay Billi Hajj Ko Chali:

Billi can't go to Hajj without a Mahram. The heck she can't even leave her house these days without a Mahram or she'll pay the price. And what's the guarantee that she won't start eating Choohay back from the Hajj? This proverb should be modified so that it makes some sense "Abay Lay! Phir Say 900 Choohay Kha Kay Billi Aur Mahram Hajj Ko Chalay!"

Aam Kay Aam, Ghutlion Kay Daam:

Did someone say IRS? Not only are you required to declare how much you made on the mangoes, but also need to declare the income you made on the Ghutlian. You can't tell IRS "Aam Khanay Say Matlab Hay Ya Pair Ginnay Say?" Then you will be audited for the number of Aam trees that you haven't declared in your return.

100 Sunaar Ki, Aik Lohar Ki:

This refers to the daily income. If Sunar keeps on saving just a little "stuff" from people's jewelry everyday, he will stay far ahead of the Lohar who is sweating in the sun hammering a worthless piece of junk.

Poori Jaati Daikhiye To Aadhi Deejiye Baant:

This is as stupid as can be! 50% is to too much to share with agencies and law enforcement when in trouble. Usually 10% is supposed to be enough and is already taken into calculations and set aside.

Gode Hari Hona:

What's so special about this one? I was in a restaurant waiting for an order of Biryani when suddenly the waiter dropped the Raita in my lap. This made my Gode totally Hari. In another incident, a kid dropped aloo bukharay ki chatni in his lap and the gode become maroon. There is a similar one equally ridiculous called "Haath

Peelay Hona!" One day in Karachi I held something very hot and burned my hand. Someone gave me Burnol and that made my Haath Peelay. Although, I don't remember if "Gode Hari Hona" occurred before "Haath Peelay Hona" or was it the other way? Anyway, who cares these days!

MAIN

This is only about Main...Main like in Main, Me, and Myself!

Main is the most important entity in the universe...at-least in Main's. As Main steps outside of Main's house, Main can see the sun revolving around Main and the moon trying to give Main a smile. When the stars twinkle, they are actually winking at Main. Breezes blow for Main and rivers flow for Main...

In English language, they have acknowledged Main's importance and have adopted the word "Main" to be used for the meaning of Central, Principal, the most important, the center-stage, the major, the focal point, the key, etc.

Every town has a street named after Main called the Main Street. It feels so nice to walk on Main Street where everybody has come just to look at Main. Main is yet to find a "Tum Street" and this proves how Main dominates all the Tums and Aaps out there.

If there's a conversation going on between a group of friends, Main can't take sides, as then Main will become like any other ordinary person. And also that Main does not have the knowledge or caliber to take a side and stick to it...but at the same time Main has to prove that Main is Main and not like "Tums"...

So Main has saved text that can be copy/pasted beautifully in any conversation:

"I think we are mature enough not to argue on petty issues like these..."

"We should not rush to a judgment based on mere facts..."

"C'mon guys, lets not fight like kids, it's time to grow-up..."

"I agree with you somewhat but not a whole lot..."

Also, Main has discovered that for a real Main look and feel, it's even better to change the topic of the conversation a whole 180 degrees, if not, at least 90 or more. So, if the thread is about "How the young Muslim generation can adopt to Islamic values in the US", Main's reply would be "A comparison of slots between Atlantic City and Vegas!" And if the topic is "Does the east-coast offer better job prospects than the west-coast or the Midwest?" Main would reply "Namaz Parho, Qabal Is Kay Tumhari Namaz Parhi Jaye!" Main loves to repeat this one specially as it refers to "Tumhari" as in "Tum" and does not point back to Main!

When Main gets into a "Tu Tu Main Main" with someone, rest assured that Main is only doing "Main Main"...Tu Tu is left for all the Thoo Thoos out there...Thoo on Tus!

Main's favorite animal is the goat...Main not only loves it's Karhai but the fact that this creature is all about Main, Main, and Main. Even when it's about to be slaughtered, it starts shouting louder Main, Main, Main...it's a lesson for everyone to stick to Main under all kinds of circumstances including knives.

The next jump for Main is to become "Hum". This requires a constant use of Main all the time and all the way until it suddenly dawns on Main that now Main is a "Hum". This happened to all kings and emperors and rulers of this world.

A Hum constantly Humming Hums, becomes the envy of everyone still stuck at Main!

MASAEL AUR UN PAY HUL

You have seen "Aap Kay Masael Aur Un kay Hul" in Friday newspapers for quite some time. The Maulana is not only rude and cruel in his answers, but he tries to push his own agenda.

Federal Agent Hazrat Allama Secular Shareef has agreed to answer some more burning questions directly from the public. His replies not only puts a Hul on the question, but rather a tractor, which makes the problem disappear and leaves a happy customer.

Q: I have a religious problem. I think Religion is problem.

A: Religion gives some problem in the beginning, but with training, it becomes OK.

Q: Maulana, I have gathered 50 Million from my own skills just for worldly pleasures. No Deeni purpose is intended from this money like Khairat, Sadaqat etc. Don't tell me I have to pay Zakat on this.

A: Zakat is levied on the money gifted by Allah. Since all this wealth was produced by your own expertise, don't fall into the Zakat pit.

Sri Lankan Dessert

Let me know if you need sound investment advice!

Q: Maulana Sahib, I have run away from my home 4 times. I ran away once with my tutor, then with my gardener, the third time with a colleague, and then with a waiter. Someone told me that in Islam, you couldn't run away more than 4 times. Also, what is the minimum "Sharaee" age for running from home?

A: Bibi, this question needs detailed explaining in person. Please visit me at Aastana Aalia after dark, I mean Isha prayers.

Q: We are a very religious family and want to know that if it's better to face the birthday cake towards Qibla before cutting? Also, what is the Islamic prayer for birthdays?

A: Even if the cake is not facing Qibla, Allah will accept your birthday, as He is Ghafoor-ur-Raheem. Always try to invite pious people on birthdays and parties who know such prayers. Our address is at the top of the column.

Q: Our uncle just died and we want to video-tape his final proceedings. What kind of background music should we use? The DVD will be sent to our relatives abroad and if they don't like the visual effects and sound track, it will be shameful for uncle's soul.

A: Usually I recommend remixes on such occasions. Any good rap mixed with a little touch of soul and hard rock flashes do the job. Also, Bhangra beats with chorus cut-ins, give you a spiritual feeling while lowering the body into the grave. My personal favorites would be:

Jawad Tehmad – Occhaya Khandana Wali Bhaag Gayee,

Ghapla Meray Dil Kay Undar.

Bharmaar – Aaja Tay Bayja Handle Tay.

Q: Hakeem Sahib, sorry...Religious Sahib, I am in a bizarre situation. My mom is dating my boyfriend. Someone told me that Islam gives some significance to parents. Should I dump my mother for my boyfriend or dump the guy for my mother. What if he dumps both of us? By the way, my mother already dumped my father. And my boyfriend dumped his old girlfriend.

A: Mashallah, Nazar-e-Bad Door, is there anyway to get a US visa quickly? Is there any Masjid over there looking for a Maulvi? Can you sponsor me?

Q: Hazrat Baray Sahib...Salam. According to Shariat, if one gives "Rishwat" or takes "Rishwat", he will go to hell. What if one arranges "Rishwat"? Please give an easy Fatwa as I am a federal employee and this is all I do. You are the 5th Maulvi I am trying.

A: Referring to my own book – Daboos Ul-Mutazalzaleen, ch. 115, page 116, para 4, line 3, in the old Islam, Rishwat was considered bad. However, as Islam has evolved, it is now considered Haqooq Ul-Ibad to exchange Rishwat.

Q: We have grown old and our four children are adults now. How much Thawab do old parents get for serving adult kids? Is it true that Islam prohibits saying even, "Boo!" to kids? Should we fold hands while in their presence? Do our hands have to be above or below the navel?

A: It is strictly forbidden for parents to even stare at kids in Islam. Even if they yell at you or scold you or give you a beating, parents have to show due respect. Islam teaches respect, manners,...etc. Hanafi parents fold their hands below the navel and Shafi parents above.

Sri Lankan Dessert

Q: How many Witar are there in the Jumah prayers?

A: What is Witar/Jumah prayers? Never spread confusion in Islam!

Q: My father died recently and I am his oldest son. Now, I want to take all what he left behind and give nothing to the rest of the kin. Is that possible? Please change the religion.

A: Fatwa forms are available for 2.5% of the total value that the Sael will get. Blank attested forms are available for a specific Hadiya as well. Jazak Allah Fid Darain!

Q: Maulana Sahib, we have a big problem. Where we live, there is Halal Meat available everywhere. We have to travel far to get good Haraam Meat. In this case, is it OK to eat Halal Meat? By the way, I also know the Kalma and consider myself a good Muslim.

A: Yes, you can eat Halal Meat in desperate cases. I eat Halal Meat myself if nothing else is available.

Q: What does Islam say about performing magic? People say that I cast spell on them when they look at me...Haay Taubah!!

A: Uf-Alalh...Bibi, this is a very complicated religious matter and needs personal correspondence. Please send two poster-size pictures of you with a return envelope and your phone number.

Q: Is water necessary to perform Wudhu?

A: You can perform Wudhu with mud, air, etc. After all, the human being is made of mud and always passing out air. Ref: Daboos Ul-Mutazalzaleen, ch. 255, page 183, para 5, line 12.

Q: I have some money and want to spend it on some good deeds. Should I spend it on myself or Hadiya it to my acquaintances? Do my acquaintances have to be poor?

A: Islam places great importance on the rights of rich people. If everyone starts looking after poor people, who will take care of the rich?

MATHS 101

This is a crash course that explains basic math terms with examples. Equally suitable for white collar, blue collar, no collar (pants only), and scholar students.

Arithmetic:

Trying to do calculations.

 example: If the bank deducts $65 and the "Hundi" is charging Rs.1.80 per Dollar, to send $3200 to Abbaji in Nazimabad, its best to tell him to wait until the next time you visit him.

Inversely Proportional:

The increase of one entity causes the decrease of other.

Example: The Pakistani Army's budget and Pakistan's area in sq. kilometers.

Directly Proportional:

The increase in one entity causes the same effect in the other.

Example: The number of police personnel and the number of crimes per day.

Arithmetic Progression:

Obtained by adding a value repeatedly to a number. Think of the rate of corruption in Pakistan.

Geometric Progression:

Obtained by multiplying a value repeatedly to a number.

Example: The increase in prices in Pakistan.

Average:

Obtained by dividing the total of measurement by the number of measurements. If 2,400 people commit suicide annually in Pakistan, on average 200 people kill themselves every month.

Mean:

The central one. Like a Mean bureaucrat in Islamabad is enjoying a central position.

Percentage:

When combined should always make up 100. Suppose a man earns Rs. 100 in a day and while going home to his family, police takes away Rs. 100. So, according to mathematics, the total earning of the police and the man is 100% + 0% = 100%. Remember, Mathematics is never wrong.

Algebra:

Trying to find the unknown. If "X" has "Y" bank accounts in "Z" countries, then how much time does Pakistan have left? And other stuff similar to this.

Take this Equation for example:

If E < I and F > R, Then D = P. If Exports are less than Imports and Foreign debt is more than the Revenue, then Democracy is in Progress.

Relational Operators:

Logical Operators. If you have Relations in higher-ups, logically you can operate easily and freely.

Variable:

Always changing. Say the voltage in a house in Karachi changes from 119 Volts to 0 Volts and then suddenly to 1100 Volts and back to 0 Volts, then the voltage is a variable.

Constant:

Always the same. When the voltage is a variable, the burnt TV, Fridge and Voltage Stabilizer are a Constant.

Geometry:

Trying to make sense out of shapes. Some shapes like Shape of economy or Shape of things to come are Shapeless. Some things are Shapeless, for every other thing there is Geometry.

Line:

Set of points. It represents things like how many more people are living below the poverty line in Pakistan?

Triangle:

Three points not willing to meet. Represents the power struggle between the President, Prime Minster and C-in-C.

Circle:

Round with no way out. Most important is the "Vicious Circle". That's when public eats-up foreign loans and the poor government has to pay them back. To pay the loans, government increases taxes and prices. Because of the exponential values, the public does not pay taxes and stops buying things. To cover the lost revenue, government takes more loans, which again the poor people eat-up.

Also, circles are what "Mere Ghareeb Hamwatno!" see when they had nothing to eat for two days, but again, how many examples you expect in a refresher course?

Oval:

Circle with a twist. Just remember "Oval Office". That's where all "calculations" are done and all "figures" come from.

Square:

Four equal sides. Remember the most important "Square One". This is the place where every government project and plan comes back to.

Rhombus:

Four sides with a tilt. This is how "Square One" looks when all official plans come back to it.

Parallelogram:

Sides always parallel to each other. An example would be the Super class and the Sweeper class.

Pentagon:

A five sided area. The Pentagon represents the desire to own the five continents of the globe.

NATIONAL BANK OF PAKISTAN – MAIN BRANCH

It was a fine morning of a very memorable day, 5th Dec. 1989, the day our N.E.D. batch had planned a Holi in the campus. Sometimes I just get nostalgic by remembering good old days of Karachi when it was a livable city and I was a part and parcel of it.

That day, I was late to join the festivities at campus because of this Funny-Kharabi. Actually, I had to submit the fee for my TOEFL exam and I needed a money order made in US funds.

I left the house early in the morning and dashed to the local National Bank in the hopes of saving time. I went to a counter where a lady was sitting playing with her hair-band. As soon as she saw me approaching, she lowered her gaze and started to tremble a little.

Of course I was wearing the most worn-out shirt and pants in my wardrobe as it was Holi that day and everyone knows what happens during Holi! But I guess that was not the reason. She just couldn't handle the sudden appearance of a young chap with harassingly good looks. I explained what I needed and she swiftly put her chadar on top of her head. With a meek voice and trembling hands she replied "Foreign Exchange branch Say Banay Ga!". Although a little disappointed, I was still trying to cope with my new personality.

Now, I had two choices; either go to the National Bank across Sir Syed Girls College in Nazimabad or head for the main branch near Tower. As it was around 9:00 in the morning, the college must have already started. Well, 12 o'clock would have been a different story but now there would be no one on the bus stop to take notice of my harassingly good looks which didn't care for costly clothing. Moreover, I did not want to hear some other excuse again. So I headed for the National Bank – Main Branch because that's the "Main branch". There goes my Holi...

When I reached Tower, I disembarked near the BCCI building and asked a person where the National Bank – Main Branch is. He advised me to walk in one direction where there were some office buildings and the most difficult to enter is the one you're looking for. I shrugged my shoulders and started walking towards that direction and then approached a yellowish structure. The building had no signs as they had been taken down for repairs. There was construction material at the front door with abundant stagnant sewer water. I felt thankful to my guide for the advice, avoided a fragile man-hole cover and entered. Inside, I encountered more Bajri studded with fresh Paan Ki Peek. Following the Paan Ki Peek trail, I came near the entrance of a big hall. As I was about to enter the hall, few live hanging wires barely missed me by a few inches. I wished that some other tall guys I know, would have visited the Main Branch at that time.

There were people with small desks and lots of registers sitting on both sides of the hall. There were heaps of Bajri wherever there was some empty space, together with cement bags. Looked like a couple of the walls were being repaired. I negotiated a few cement blocks and clutch wire rounds on the floor and reached a table. The guy sitting at that table probably went to bed in the same clothes. That really helped me stop feeling guilty-conscious. He made an oval-like shape with his mouth and moved his chin up to prevent the Paan Ki Peek from falling on the register, which would have made little difference anyway. "Qiya Qawaam Hai!" he said in a voice drenched in Paan juices. I acknowledged that his choice of Qawaam is excellent as I can smell it right where I am standing. "Qiya Masala Hai!", he continued. I again confirmed that his taste in Paan and its Masalajaat is royal. He moved his head to the right, relieved his entire load on the ample Bajri and asked "Amaan Kiyon Tapkay Ho? Kiya Kaam Hai? Masla Kiya Hai?". I replied "Ji Bank Draft Banwana Hai!". He pointed towards two guys and said nothing further.

They were standing close to the wall. I approached the first one and said "Ji Bank Draft Banwana Hai!". He replied: "Aray To Banwalo! Hum Kiya Karen!". Then I noticed that he had a "Karandi" in his hand and was actually plastering the wall. The other guy quickly moved towards me, sprayed a fresh load of red fluid on the Bajri and explained that he was just checking this Mistari's work. "Hum Banaay Daitay Hain Tumhara Draft!".

He took me to his desk and I finally had a chance to sit down. He asked me all the whats and whys and as I stated the amount and beneficiary, he slapped his forehead (luckily not mine).
"Aray...Pahlay Kiyon Nahin Batlaya, Hum Faqat Rupay Kay Draft Banaya Kartay Hain!". I asked him who makes US dollar drafts. "Woh Koi Aur Banatay Hain!". Then, he suddenly felt discomforted, stood-up and started walking in one direction. I thought that he finally realized my agony and wanted to take me to the actual person. I followed him till we reached a narrow, dark corridor and just before entering a smelly room, he heard my footsteps and looked behind: "Yahan Kahan Ayee Ga! Eee To Toilet Hay! Bhajjan Mian To Huwaan Hain!"

At last some luck! If I can just find Bhajjan Mian, I can be the owner of a US bank draft. I started hiking on the Bajri and Paan trail and was back in the hallway. A person looked at me and called me with a wave of hand. I approached him. He was the first person whom I found smiling. He started listening to me and interrupted me with a big grin and told me that he just won Rs. 200,000 in prize bonds. A Maulana sitting on the next desk retorted that money is not his as the prize bond actually belongs to his wife. Before the matter could get worse, I asked for Bhajjan Mian. The Maulana pointed to a dude sitting, almost camouflaged by a heap of Bajri.

When I went behind the heap, I could see a dude sitting, wearing a suit. Wow! Finally luck had struck me. I approached him and told him what I needed. He told me go to the window, deposit the equivalent in Rupees, get him the receipt and a photo copy of my TOEFL form. When I was frolicking towards the window, he shouted and asked me about the amount. I told him the amount. He said "Bachat Ho Gayee! Agar Kaheen $200 Say Jiyada Amount Ho To Phir Chaudhri Sahab Hi Bana Payen Gay Aur Woh Gaaon Gaye Huay Hain. Fasal Ko Paani Waani Laganay!".

I paid the money at the counter and gave him the receipt and the photocopy. He checked the amount: "Nau Sau Nabbay Rupay Aur Aik Giyara Paisay!" He then started calling for a "Launda".

Finally the 'Launda' appeared and sat down at one of the two typewriters lying beside Bhajjan Mian's desk. I gave him the beneficiary's name to be written on the draft on a piece of paper: "TOEFL (Test of English as a foreign language)". Launda was constantly chewing a bubblegum and looking at the construction work going on. He seldom looked at the keyboard or the stuff being typed. I was jealous of his typing skills and felt very bad when I realized my own typing speed. The draft was handed to me. Thank God, it was over!!

As I was about to leave Bhajjan Mian's cabin, I looked at the draft, and it read: "TOEFL (Test of Enfish as a foreign language)" My heart started sinking. I went back to Bhajjan Mian and complained. He looked at the draft and burst out at the Launda. After a really bad scolding with stuff like "Abay Spelling Bhi Nahin Atay To Yahan Kiya Karwanay Ata Hai...etc." He took the draft, made corrections by hand and gave it back to Launda. This time the Launda took 10 minutes to type. Bhajjan Mian pulled out the draft himself from the typewriter, cross-checked it with his corrections, signed it and gave it back to me, smiling. I looked at the beneficiary: "TOEFL (Test of English in a foreign language)". He winked at me victoriously, "Bas Kaam Theek Ho Gaya To Samjho Sab Theek Hai".

My floating heart started sinking again. Will the TOEFL people ignore the "in" for an "as". Should I try to erase the "in" with a razor blade and try to make it "as"? Should I go to Bhajjan Mian and Launda again? I couldn't do it. I just couldn't do anything. The most fun day of my life was already ruined.

I left the National Bank – Main Branch, went to the Post Office – Main Branch and dropped the form with the draft. When I reached the campus, it was past 12:00 and the major celebration was over. However, I was spotted quickly. A couple of friends got a hold of me and with a big splash, threw me in the fountain!

The TOEFL guys must have had the last laughs but they ignored the spellings and processed my form. But this story doesn't end here so bare with me just a tad bit more. A year later, I was starting my studies in Michigan with four other batch mates. It was our 1st day on the campus. One of our friends, Maulana, was told to report to the foreign students' advisor. As we were fresh from N.E.D., with a group-like mentality, we all accompanied him to the advisor's office.

As we sat in front of her, the advisor asked for Maulana and then started gazing at him with a big grin. Then she leaned forward smiling, and whispered "Will you please marry me?" This came like a tornado. It was our 4th day in the US and a blonde in tight skirt was already proposing to a Desi. Maulana had an aghast on his face. It looked like, "Yeh To Seat Pay Hi Faarigh Ho Jayen Gay!" Then, she pulled his file out and out came a bank draft. The bank draft had a stamp "National Bank of Pakistan – Main Branch", duly signed by Bhajjan Mian and was made out for $25,000. The actual processing fee was $25.

She mentioned that when the university received the bank draft, they ignored it and processed the application anyway as the winter semester was about to start. But she chuckled that all her life, she wanted to marry a millionaire, from a far-off land.

We paid the $25 and as we were heading for the stairs, I kept on thinking: It's true that Americans do ignore things sometimes but how come a harassingly good looking guy gets ignored in favor of a millionaire.

NEW MINISTRIES

I would like to suggest some new portfolios for the new ministers:

Minister for Graves:

First, there should be a minister for Kafan/Dafan. People killed due to lawlessness, bombings, military action, starvation, suicides, accidents, consuming impure water, and pure bullets deserve to be buried honorably. A minister can look after this in a more dignified way.

His Oath must include "Namaz-e-Janaza". He can be given contracts for allotting graves to people...of course, corner plots will cost a little "more".

Minister for Downplaying:

This ministry will take on the arduous task of making sure that every catastrophe and calamity (natural or manmade) is downplayed for the sake of keeping people at ease.

For example, the Downplaying Minister will advise the Media - "I think that only 2000...500...120...50...40...aaaaaa...maybe 30, 19, 11 or just 5, 3, 1 people have died!" whenever 2 or more trains collide or an earthquake hits a city. Or maybe an official announcement can go like "We will get rid of load-shedding in 300...180...53...I mean 41 or Hosakta Hay 21...aaaaa...10...Yaani Kay ...7, 5, 3, 2...or may be less years!" (Applause!)

Minister for Fast Foods:

We definitely need a minister for nutrition to ensure that the food prices only pinch the poor and don't rise beyond the reach of rich people, so rich people do not have to fly to Dubai or London for a good lunch or dinner.

An experienced hand from the KFC or McDonald's should be preferred. Successful importers of "Jhatka" confirmed as "Halal" from outside will be given preferences.

Minister for Renaming:

We need a Renaming minister to rename all bridges, hospitals, airports, and mental hospitals after some living or dead folks.

He should also rename some parties, for instance: Muslim League "Qaaf", "Gaaf", "Laam", "Chay", "Noon", and Pakistan Paidal Party, etc. to give them a touch of class.

Minister for Lame Excuses:

This has to be the most dynamic minister of all. He/She/It will be needed whenever the government does something it was not supposed to do or doesn't do something it was supposed to do. This, to me, is a 24/7 responsibility and the minister should always carry a pager around. As soon as the pager beeps and the incoming message spills the beans, this guy should start chirping:

"When our honorable president asked Sara Palin for a "Hug", he was actually asking the way to the bathroom as he needed to do Number 2".

"When foreigners bomb our areas they are actually helping us by leveling the mountains and making the terrain more accessible".

"People complain that Aata, Milk, Ghee, Meat, and Medicines are out of reach; however, our government has made every effort possible that Sunlight, Moonlight, Sand, Air, and Sea Water are readily available to the masses" .

Lastly, we need an advisor to keep on paging the minister above.

NISHAN-E-GATHER

As always, the President of Pakistan will be distributing awards on Pakistan's Dependence Day. The prizes are given to recognize the "Note-ables" in a Cere-Money full of fang and flare. Let's checkout some of the awards:

Nissan-e-Gather:

The highest coveted award always earned by military as no one else comes close. The more they "Gather-Together", the higher are the chances of getting one. The award is given when top ranking army officers put other's lives in danger and go beyond and far-away from the call of duty to perform heroin operations. Other competitors for Nishan-e-Gather are "Caror Commanders" who put their life in arms way and get involved in commissioning to protect the country from de-commissioning.

Hilal-e-Phurrat:

This award is bestowed for the highest demonstration of gallantry. The medal can be given to both uniformed and un-informed recipients. Just as some officers got "Phurr" from the battle front in 1971, so did the politicians. Since, most of the ex. Prime Sinisters and Wuzra-e-Kaalaa have fled the country, the award will be received on their behalf by the ones who shared the half.

Sitara-e-Khijalat:

This Sitara will go to the Bura-Cracy. When our secretaries and advisors meet the IMF/World Bank officials, they are persistent in begging and consistent in Khijalat. The prize goes to the Bura-Cracy and the price goes to the Public. The Khijalat also takes place when an ex-MNA goes to his constituency to get re-elected. But this is short-termed as it would soon turn into Khibaasat after the Illactions.

Tamgha-e-Tawalat:

The feudal lords of Pakistan are the main recipients of this Tamgha. Pakistan is proud to be the only country remaining in the universe to be self-sufficient in Feudalism. We not only provide a sanctuary to the extinct feudals but also have the longest record on earth of their mating, breeding, preying, and decaying. If you would like to see a Feudal Safari, just wait for the next assembly to take oath.

Quaid-e-Azam Award:

This is the most beloved award in Pakistan as it's a true sign of love for the founder of the nation. The government has printed pictures of Baba-e-Qaum and numbered them from five to thousands. Those who collect more pictures with bigger numbers are considered the most patriotic. The President will hand out many envelopes full of such pictures to patriot Pakistanis on Dependence Day. The Press always gets impressed when such pictures change hands. The act of Baba-e-Qaum's pictures changing hands even changes the administration.

Presidential Award for Husne Paar-Kardagi:

It's a special award for foreign account holders. This award will be "handled-out" to the Pakistanis who have taken extra effort to boost the world's economy. These Pakistanis, having a global vision and thinking above and beyond the geographical limits of country, have transferred funds "Saat Samandar Paar". This is a safe investment as all the money has gone in a safe.

Muqaddar Ka Chuqandar:

This is a title given to any common Pakistani. The Pakistan government acknowledges the role played by the public for the betterment and welfare of the government and wants to bestow this title. The awards committee proposed handing out half a pound of Chuqandars to every Pakistani, but the Finance Minister informed them that this would put an unnecessary burden on the national exchequer. The Finance Minister has been awarded Rs. 1 Billion for his timely advice and the title "Chuqandar Ka Sikander".

Wifetime Achievement Award:

Most of the VIPs come in this cadre. Some have 8 official wives while others have other official's wives. There is no need to buy the cow if milk is available in market. So just rent the cow. VIPs also use the wives recycle program, which conserves energy and is surroundings friendly. However, the award will be given to the VIP with the longest innings and still having the bat-in-hand.

Fakhri

ONE GOOD NEWS

Last week, things were slow at work (or maybe I finished stuff pretty quick). So, it was mid morning and there was nothing much to do. I wanted to kill some time untill lunch. What better way than to browse the newspapers and check-out things in my beloved country...of course, I mean Pakistan...not India!

So, here I am browsing the newspapers (for free) and sipping exotic coffee (of course, free!). I felt a little esteemed...kind of VIP. My mood elevated...is this what the Prime Minister and other dignitaries do in their offices?

I felt like a Royal brat. The main page..."Karachi Main Fasaadaat main 20-25 Afraad Maar Diye Gay". OK, that was a little sudden. I kept looking... "Aur 5 Mazeed Maar Diyegaye"..."Terrorists have entered the country and will act at the appropriate time!"..."Pakistan lost by eight wickets"....."Power rates to go up by 9%"..."No power in Karachi for most of the day"...I think the taste of the coffee (although it's free) didn't seem that good. I added some more sugar, took a deep breath, and looked at some other news.

"Girls school blown-up in Bannu!"..."Zahreela Halwa Khanay Say 30 Afraad Beemar Hogaye"..."Drone Attacks Ka Daayra Pooray Mulk Main Phailaaya Jayega!"..."Baghair American Aid Kay Hum Bhookay Mar Jayengay". OK, I think the building's cooling system was malfunctioning as it started feeling hot. I asked the guy in my neighboring cube about it. He was looking at the stock prices and reading US economic prospects and he readily agreed. The guy in the cube across from me was checking his mail. He shrugged his shoulders and said that the cooling system was working fine.

My mood was now serious. I realized that this must be how the VIPs feel when they read the news and it shows on their face when they are in public. I carried on trying to find some good news that would make my day. "Pakistan Aik Dahshatgard Mulk Hay Aur World Cup 2011 Ki Mazebaani Kay Qaabil Nahin Hay"..."Provincial Cabinet Ki Taadaad 65 Hogayee Hay"..."Dakaiti Main Mazahmat Par 3 Afraad Halaak!"..."Manawan Police Center Pay Hamlay Kay Mujrimon Ka Taa Haal Pata Nahin Chal Nhin Chal Saka"..."Musheer-e-Daakhla Ab Wazeer-e- Daakhla Ho Gaye Hain!"

My manager sent me an IM asking for something. I changed my status from "Online" to "Busy". Can't they just leave me alone for a while? Why do I have to reply to everything? Why isn't my chair comfortable? And, this computer totally sucks!

For no reason, my mood became desperate. But, I didn't lose hope yet. All the bad things happen in mega cities. I believe small towns and cities are peaceful and serene. I reclined in the chair a little bit and went on to the small town news section to find that one good news!

Sukkur – "Expired Injection Laganay Say 3 Bachay Chal Basay!" Multan – "2 Roze Qabal Ighwa Honay Wali Bachi Ki Naash Nahar Kinaray Mili".

Jhang – "School Ki Building Girnay Say Teacher Samait 4 Students Halaak!"
Bonair – "10 Security Ahalkaar Ighwa Kar Liye Gay!".
Shekhupoora – "Clerks Nay 6 Maah Say Tankhuwah Naa Dainay Pay Khood Sozi Ki Dhamki Day Di!"
Jacobabad – "Chandio Qabeelay Nay Lashaari Qabeelay Kay 7 Afraad Haalaak Aur 9 Zakhmi Kar Diye!"

The cramping in my stomach could have been caused by the omelet that I had for breakfast. Or, maybe the air quality at work isn't great and is causing me nausea. My wife said that after 40, you need to keep an eye on your blood pressure so, it could just be my age that is making me feel hot all over. Depression is actually a physical ailment so, who knows that I have a chemical imbalance in my head and need to start Prozac.

But, if I just had one good news!...It would fix everything...One good news from the country that I love. It would elevate me and make me useful again...I asked Allah for help and looked at village news...small places...small problems!

"Sasti Sharab Peenay Say 5 Aadmi Halaak"..."Private Jail Main Qaid Mazaron Nay Bhook Hartaal Kardi"..."Nozaida Bachon Ko Polio Kay Qatray Nahin Pilay Jaa Sakay"..."Aadmi Aur Jaanwar Aik Hi Talaab Say Paani Pi Rahay Hain!"

Stubborn as I am, I won't let go! God has to help me right now and right here. I need one good news to get through...just one and not two! I opened the editorial columns page to see some ray of light... some hope!..."Tauba Ka Waqt Guzar Chuka Hay!"..."Gandum Ki Fasal Kiyon Tabah Hui?"..."Bachon Main Nasha Karna Ka Ruhjaan"..."Logo! America Say Daro!"..."Khawateen Ko Bhi Talaaq Ka Haq Milna Chahiye!"

My wife called, "Are you coming home for lunch?" I don't think I was rude to her but don't know why she hung-up. I was staring at the screen. How could God let me down? I felt like the *Titanic's* captain. Without knowing it, I clicked the latest news section again...Aah! And there it was...the one good news I've been waiting for...Allah (SWT) never lets one's prayers go unanswered...with a thankful heart and tearful eyes...I read the news:

"Sadar-e-Mumlikat 10 Mulkon Kay Dauray Pay Rawana Ho Gaye!"

Cheerful and whistling with joy, I stood up a new person and headed home for lunch.

PAKISTANI INNOVATIONS

I have been criticized before for not finding anything good regarding our country. This time, I want to prove my critiques wrong as I've researched hard and found out that Pakistan leads the rest of the globe in the following innovations. Take a look:

Mobile Phone Recycle:

Pakistan has the world's biggest mobile phone recycle network. You buy a new phone and as soon as you leave the store, folks will approach you and will gladly take the phone away where it will be recycled back to the store for the next customer.

If you do not agree with the recycling efforts, they will gladly take your life and recycle it back to the right owner.

Stealth Technology:

The western powers including Russia are still struggling in this respect. They haven't come-up with a single truly stealth aircraft or vessel where as we dominate the world in Stealth equipment. An ex-admiral acquired submarines that were so stealthy that not only enemies but also our own navy couldn't detect them. This stealth technology is the one big fear that keeps the enemies away from us.

Also, the enemies realize that they do not need to try to destroy Pakistan...Pakistan already has a government!

Food Processing:

We have the most innovative food processing facilities in the world. As an example, if you pick-up a rice bag in US and check the ingredients, you would be disappointed to find just "Rice". That's all the developed countries have to offer? If you take a rice bag in Pakistan and check it out, you'll find: "Silica, Sedimentary rocks, grounded granite, coarse crushed stone, fine beach sand, powdered glass and yes, some rice!" Now, that's what I call indigenous food processing. This kind of food processing also serves to keep the population under control.

The government also knows that red peppers, for example, are bad for your health. So, they are allowing it to be mixed-up with powdered bricks to be more healthy and satisfying.

Environment-Friendly Energy:

OK, I proclaim – Pakistan leads the world and any other race in the universe, if there are any, in this aspect. As the world is still using the age-old electricity day and night, Pakistan has totally abandoned the use of this polluting and dangerous means of energy. We rely solely on solar energy to work in the day and moonlight to go through the night.

Also, Pakistani folks use wind energy for cooling, if it's blowing, and thank God that they still have it.

Anti-Aging Miracles:

As I said before, we lead the world in a few things and this is one of them, as it has Pakistani patent rights. This miraculous technology is one that allows both father and son to be playing in the same under-19 team. And, it enables an army general to remain chief of army staff for 12 years as the more he uses it, the younger he gets.

Forget all those useless anti-aging creams etc. as our Desi technology not only keeps you young forever, but also keeps on changing your birth certificate to go with it. The world can't beat that!

Transportation Techniques:

Remember the Star Trek's transporters and the way they moved stuff without leaving a trace! Again, I feel ecstatic to announce that Pakistanis have mastered this technology. Some 600 people and 60 billion dollars have been transported out of the country without leaving a trace. This technology is now becoming a day to day thing that, as soon as you deposit some foreign currency in any local bank...Poof!! it's transported immediately to accounts in Dubai, London and New York.

The world thinks this is plain "magic"; however, we know that it's just one of the technology marvels of 21st century.

Matric System:

The so called "advanced" world is still far behind in implementing the Matric system in which Pakistan is, once again, a world leader. The proof: President – Matric Pass, Cabinet – Matric Fail. Most of the VIPs – Matriculate at best and are not willing to go any further as that would violate the whole Matric system.

POLY-TICKELLY INCORRECT

A look at some of the VVIPs who could have been appointed as the President of Pakistan.

ABU-JAHAL:

Yes, a good name to start the list. Could have been a perfect Wadera president that Legharis or Mazaris would envy. However, it's said that this "father of ignorance" was able to read and write complete sentences that made sense. Nowadays, we have revolutionized the presidency to new heights and this quality is just obsolete.

He had some other demerits like feeding the hungry and keeping promises...well...let's not then waste time on this misfit and move on.

ABU-LAHAB:

Yep, being a staunch enemy of Islam puts him at the top of the candidate list; however, he had many negatives attributed to him that easily fail him. Drenched in patriotism and super-national fever, he would be an utter failure in the War on Error.

Wouldn't tolerate Drone attacks...His false national pride would never allow countrymen to be sold to a foreign invader...Would never allow FBI cells...just not his type. So, we happily denounce him as the President of Pakistan. Let's move on.

PHAROAH:

All along, I thought that this would be an excellent choice. I mean, at least you expect someone to proclaim Divineness before you select him as the president of Pakistan and yes, all the arrogance that comes handy. Although Pharaoh would also be the best choice for Prime Minister, Governor, any Minister, Advisor, Additional Advisor, Secretary, Chairman, Head of any Department, Politician, Army Officer, Bureaucrat, SHO, Upper Division Clerk, Lower Division Clerk, Naib Nazim, WAPDA supervisor, KESC line man, Patwaari...Oh My God!

But still we cannot nominate Pharaoh. Right before he was drowning, he realized that the sovereignty belongs to someone else...What a shame! What a disappointment! He could have at least learned something from our Mard-e-Momin, Mard-e-Haq who may still be challenging God's sovereignty...even without the denture!

NIMROD:

OK, this time we may be up to something. This guy had guts. He proclaimed to be the Chief Executive...I mean...the God. He used to tell Ibrahim (AS)..."Main Darta Warta Nahin Hoon"; however, the poor guy couldn't even handle one single bug up in his brain...Pathetic!

He should feel embarrassed to learn that the Presidents of Pakistan have been ruling the country with brains infested with bugs, germs, insects and what not. This is what you call guts!

HAJJAJ BIN YOUSUF:

A good choice for killing scores of innocent Muslims and could be a role model for Busharraf. However, Afia Siddiqi would have long been brought back from captivity or, even worse, would never have been handed over to the outsiders. This automatically disqualifies him from becoming the President.

SHADDAAD:

Shaddaad was an utter failure. Couldn't even enter Aiwaan-e-Sadar, I mean, his paradise. All the fine foods, delicate women, European wines...oops...those medieval alcohols and Armani suits...oops again ..those old Yemeni robes kept on waiting and he just died helplessly.

To be a President, you need to be able, to not only enter the paradise, but keep on clinging to it. No, no, we can't nominate failures like him.

QAROON:

Better be nominated as Minister of Investment. What a moron! Couldn't take care of just a little money...Had to put it on camel backs for the entire world to watch!

Our Presidents not only have 10 times the money, but it's so beautifully placed that even earth has no clue what to swallow this time.

IBLEES:

OK, now Iblees is the top choice that everyone would agree with...right? Behind every sinister plan...Promoting evil...Prohibiting good...Making false promises...Showing "Sabz Baagh"...Making people fight with each other...Making sure everyone is doing as much evil in as little time as possible...Wow! What more can you ask for in a president?

So, is Iblees is the ultimate choice and the best suitable president for Pakistan?...Alas...he has no accounts in Dubai and Switzerland...Never owned Bambino cinema...Never had a desire to embrace Sarah Palin...Never said "Pakistan Khapay".

Tera Pakistan Hay Na Mera Pakistan Hai

Yeh Us Ka Pakistan Hai Jo Sadar-e-Pakistan Hai

SAEEN MUHNJO NRO

NRO, NRO Aur Sirf NRO...

Imported Suit Main Jachta Hoon
Awam Say Aaj Kal Bachta Hoon
Sara Mulk Mujhpay Waaro!
Saeen Munhjo NRO!

BB Ka Naam Leta Jaoon
UNO ki Duhai Deta Jaaon
Jamhooriat Jamhooriat Roze Pukaro!
Saeen Munhjo NRO!

Dollar Ki Aid Milti Jaye
Meri Baachen Khilti Jaye
Khao Piyo Aur Dakaro!
Saeen Munhjo NRO!

Economy Chahay Fail Hojaye
Mulk Ka Chahay Tail Hojaye
Qarza Charhao, Mat Utaro!
Saeen Munhjo NRO!

Dushmanon Say Mujhay Bachao
Opposition Ko Dafa Karao
Jitnay Chahay Bomb Maro!
Saeen Munhjo NRO!

Dahshartgard Agaye Hain
Wahshatgard Chaa Gaye Hain
Bahar Kay Fauji Yahan Utaro!
Saeen Munhjo NRO!

America Hamesha Saccha Hay!
India Sab Say Acha Hay!
Pakistan Ko Goli Maro!
Saeen Munhjo NRO!

SECULAR PHONES

Grrreeeeeetings.....SecPhone presents "Secular Phones". Checkout our host of features compared to the other "Fundamental Phones".

- No Activation Fees! The Secular Phone is automatically activated as soon as you leave the Fundamental Service Area.

- No eavesdropping and call monitoring like the Fundamental phones. The problem with Fundamental phones is that people who are old subscribers (like your parents or elders) try to keep an eye on your phone usage. No such stupid things happen here. With the Secular phone, you can hook-up to who ever and whenever you want.

- Anti-Static design: The Fundamental phones have way too much static. When there is a need to adapt to new kinds of phone usage, all you hear is "Loud Noise". Our sec phones are by design "Hush-Up".

- Light & Cheap: The Fundamental phones are bigger than life and carry so much extra weight, so are way too expensive. They are a problem for our dynamic customers as they stick-out in every situation. Our Secular phones are so much lighter and smaller that they can easily fit into any circumstances.

- No FCC Regulations: No FCC regulations apply to Secular phones. No bandwidths are prohibited and no frequencies are "sacred".

- Must be 18 years of age or older to subscribe to our service but we will tell you how to beat that.

- $29.99/Month gives you unchecked access for 65-70 years. Sorry, nothing works after the customer's global positioning changes.

- Free Weak-ends: We know your weaknesses...so we have included all your weak-ends in the service package. You can use the Sec phone however you want to.

- Risk Free Usage: Unlike the Fundamental phones; you don't have to enter a legal contract to start using the special features. In-fact, you can continue using the Sec Phone throughout your user life just by paying a minimal usage fee.

- Bye One, Get One Three: In the Secular Phones package, as soon as you say bye to a phone-set, you can acquire thirteen other phones without any obligation. No questions asked.

For more details call 1-800-SECPHONE or visit www.SecularPhones.com.

SHAHEED-E-BUSINESS

This happened about 18 - 20 years back ago when I was working in PIA. Shahenshah welder was working in the house trying to fix some door grills and windows. Shahenshah was a blacksmith in his 50s and was quite hard working.

One day, I came home from the airport and my mother told me that Gattu is dead and Shahenshah hasn't come to work today. She said that I should go to Gattu's funeral today as it's to be held after Asar prayers.

My father was out of town so he couldn't come with me. I immediately headed for Malir which was about 45-50 minutes from my house. While driving, I was sad and shocked, and thinking about Shahenshah and his young son. Gattu was about 18-20 yrs. old and a school throw-out (in his own words).

He would sometimes come to help his dad and his job would be to hit the chisel with the "Ghan". But most of the time he would be looking around, chewing pan, asking me about air-hostesses in PIA and "Kaun Kitna Tore Raha Hay?" His father had to insult Gattu's mother repeatedly before he would focus on the work again. Poor boy...I kept on thinking...don't know what happened to him...Gattu was too young to die!

I reached Malir just at Asar time. I parked the car in the street and rushed to the Masjid. After the prayer, they brought out Gattu's body amid tears and sobbing and put it down for Namaz-e-Janazah. The Imam Sahib was about to come out when I noticed that the dead body was lying at a 45 degrees angle with the Saff. All Janazahs that I had seen were always put parallel to the line of prayer, however this one was pointing somewhere else.

Compelled with the intent to show my brilliance, I asked one person to help me fix this issue so that we both can straighten the Janazah. He hesitated a bit but then agreed. As we were about to accomplish this task, someone put his hand on my shoulder. I looked back and a Buzurg told me in a cold voice, "Baahar Kay Dikhay Ho, Warna Youn Ungli Na Tortay!" The chill of the voice froze me in my tracks. I realized then and there that I was alone in a foreign territory and it's better to just shut up.

After the burial, I desperately wanted to ask Shahenshah about Gattu's death. He was looking grief-stricken and weak. He urged me to go to his house and have some tea before leaving. I couldn't refuse even though it's mission impossible for me to go a mourning family and try to console them. On the way to his house, I learned that some Pathan guy shot Gattu in the chest and the skinny boy didn't take long to breathe his last.

As expected, everyone had red eyes in that small house. I sat down in a corner against the wall. People were sitting in small groups and the topic was Gattu and that merciless Pathan. Shahenshah welder entered and sat near me. He was looking more composed by now. A sobbing girl brought me some tea and Namak-Paray and said, "Hamaray Gattu Bhaiyya Shaheed Ho Gaye!" I threw the standard consolation line, "Shahenshah Bhai...Bohat Dukh Hua Gattu Kay Inteqaal Ka!" Shahenshah sighed and uttered, "Aray Saali Itni

Purani, Chal Kaisay Gayee?" I didn't get it! A guy sitting next to him said, "Meray Ko Yeh Batao Shahenshah Bhai! Gattu Wali Kiyon Nahin Chali?" Shahenshah said, "Hajar Baar Bola Tha! Itni Jaldi Widdaal (withdrawal) Na Kara...Sahar Kay Halaat Garbar Hain!...Woh Sunay Hi Na!".

"Kiya Gattu bank Say Paisay Nikalwany Gaya Tha?" I asked. A guy stared at me, "Lo Ji...Phir Kiya Tumharay Ghar Jata Paisa Nikalwany?" I think a Namak-Para got stuck in my throat and I gulped a big sip to push it down. Shahenshah continued, "Abay Us Ko Bola Tha Naya Business Hay...Shtart Main Time Lagay Ga! Jaldi Na Macha...Yeh Larka Maan Kay Na Diya!"

It started coming to me. Gattu had started some new business and went to the bank for a withdrawl and some armed Pathan shot him...probably was trying to rob him. Suddenly, there was some hustle and bustle outside. Someone reported, "15 ½ Ki Mobile Ayee Hay!" Shahenshah went outside and came back in 10 minutes. "Haram Ka Bol Riya Hay...Is Bari to Mar Gaya...Pichlay Kaun Dega?...Main Nay Bola, Sub Inspector Say Jaa Kay Lay Le To Daphay Ho Gaya!".

Shahenshah shook his head in disbelief. "Bhala Batao, Gattu Ko Bola Tha Malir Say Widdaal Na Kara...Heeyan Acha Business Nahin Hay...Thora Aagay Ja...Zara Haath Pare Maar...Aur Who Saala Lay Bhi Gaya repeater!" A voice came from opposite wall, "Shahenshah bhai...Bachay Ko KK Hi De Detay"..."Woh to Mujjan Bhayya Lay Gaye hain Hyderabad...Abhi Tak Hueen Hay". I was totally surprised at this, "Gattu Repeater Lay Kay Paisay Nikalwanay Gaya Tha? Yahan Kay Haalaat Itnay Kharab Hain??" This time it was one of the guests, "Sahenshah Bhaiyya...Ab Kay Mobile Aaway To In Ka Pata Day Di Jiyo".

It's not easy to describe the feeling of being insulted and scared at the same time. However, any Pakistani can relate to it who has faced US immigration. Shahenshah asked one of the mourners who had oil and grease stains on his clothes, "Pilot ...Tu Nay Yeh Kiya Checking Ki Thi?" Pilot looked pathetic. He stammered, "Shahenshah Bhai...Quran Uthwalo...3 Dafa Main Nay Khood Check Kiya...Dheela Pathan Guard Tha Aur Gun Bhi Kuaid-e-Ajam Kay Jamanay Ki Thi...Andar Branch Main 2-3 Banday Bhi Set Thay...Meray Khayal Say Gattu Ghabra Gaya Hoga...Us Kaafir Kay Bachay Guard Nay Pahlay Chala Di". I could hear a woman crying inside the house, "Aray Meray Bachay Ka Abhi To Business Shuroo Hua Tha...Us Kameenay Pathan Nay Maar Dala...Mera Bacha Rozi Pay Mara Gaya!...Shaheed Ho Gaya!".

There wasn't anything left to know now. I wanted to press the "turbo button" and be out of there. I looked at Shahenshah to ask permission to leave. He looked at me and said "Aap Kaa Kaam Bhi Beech Main Hay!" "Koi Baat Nahin!" "Aap Ki To Grill Bhi Moti Wali Hay! Saala Koi Tore Kar Bhi Nahin Aasakay". A voice emerged, "Acha! Paisay Walay Hi Lagwaten Hay Aisi Cheezen!" Shahenshah said, "To Aur Kiya! Inka To Yeh Bara Ghar Hay! Khood PIA Main Hain! Kitna Tore Laitay Ho?"

No one noticed that I suddenly needed to make Wudhu again. I replied that it's getting late and I need to get home soon. I told Shahenshah that he doesn't need to come back to work soon and to take his time. He replied sadly, "Welding Main Aaj Kal Bachta Kiya Hay...Sonch Rahay Hain Kay Apna Koi Business Shtaart Kar Lain!"

I found my car and don't know how, reached home in 25 minutes. Told my mom that Shahenshah welder will not be coming anymore as he will be starting his new business and we need to find another welder.

SOME USEFUL INNOVATIONS

In the 21st century, when technology is advanced enough, why don't we come-up with new inventions for our dear country? Instead of trying to improve Pakistan, maybe the way out is to further improve technology and deploy it in our motherland. Please, as a national duty, add to this list.

GOO{D} GOVERNANCE GOGGLES:

Please read carefully – '**D**' is silent. This is not a new idea though, as it has been in long time use by VIPs all over the country. But we want it made available to the poor {m}asses ('m' is silent) as well. The device would look like green colored goggles that, when put-on, will fully cover the eyes, ears and nose. The device should be turned on while stepping out of the house and kept on during the entire tourage.

Now, one will start appreciating the Goo{d} ('d' is silent) done by the government as all will appear "Hara! Hara!" The Liyari River will appear as if honey is flowing in it and Gujar Naala will look like Chashma-e-Tasneem from Heaven. Birds would be larking on rose bushes that used to be garbage heaps and musk would be spreading from what used to be rotten stray animals. People would be hugging each other lovingly and the police would be smiling at kids. Gone will be the Pollution, noise and the traffic hazards and sidewalks will have red carpets on them.

You won't see any beggars including police and rangers, and the flies, rodents and pests would be replaced by dancing peacocks and frolicking deers. Of course, municipality would look so efficient as if it's cleaning after each peacock and deer. No one homeless, no one dying on the road, no one jobless – only smiling people with all the bounties that heaven can envy.

Note: Remember to take off the goggles while entering home, otherwise Begum Sahib would start looking like from heaven and this would mean more "Kharcha".

SALUTE-O-HELMET:

This is an innovation for our beloved armed forces. All the helmets, barrettes, and caps will be fitted with an automatic saluting robotic hand. The hand will be battery operated and will be saluting at a rate of 22-24 salutes a minute. The hand could be made revolving 360 degrees as you can have a senior officer standing right behind you. In fact both left and right hands could be attached to the helmet saluting and circling in opposite directions.

Solar powered Salute-O-Helmets are a plus as Chinese batteries run out very quickly. This would be a big relief for our soldiers at the front. What happens now is that right at the moment when the enemy is shelling and bombarding, everybody keeps on saluting everyone else. In this frenzy, sometimes soldiers start saluting the enemy. The Salute-O-Barret will not only keep both hands of the soldier free but will also not let anything happen to the dignity of the officers around.

RATE-O-DISPLAY:

This is concerning a mammoth problem that the entire nation is facing. You enter a government office to get something illegal done, like having residential water connection. The Sahib is sitting in his chair, smiling, reading Film ads/Zaroorat-Rishta etc. and having tea. Now, you tell him the boring story with trying to add Allah/Rasool Wasta and mentioning your five little kids. Sahib's mood turns serious as you are trying to involve divine personalities in illegal things. Also, Sarkar told you to have two kids; how come you need water for five? Serious mood means that this is Sahib's "Rozgar" time. A million people have been deceived by the Sarkari mood and often end-up paying more than what was Sahib's Rate.

There should be electromagnetic devices planted on the foreheads of Sarkar that would have the readouts for the "Guzur Auqat" that Sahib is used to. You might be tempted to paying 50,000 while his Excellency might do it for only 40,000. This would take out the haggling part from offices and would also relieve from the horrible consequences of "Jo Dil Main Aye De Dain!!" As haggling can be done only in private, the Awam have to wait for their turn one after the other.

Now, just imagine. Sahib is sitting, smiling, reading Budget-Khasara and having tea facing 10 Meray Aziz Hamwatno. He looks at one Aziz Hamwatan and instantly the read-out flashes "35,000". He again looks to the next one and he sees "40,000" on government's forehead. It's so simple. More advanced Korean made Rate-O-Meter would give a timeline also for the job like "50,000 – next week / 25,000 – six months".

HARAM-O-METER:

The Haramometer will tell the Haram eaten so far and the future Haram storing capacities. The Haram-o-meter will be like any ordinary thermometer (may be a little longer) and could be inserted from either opening. The concerned party would not mind its usage, as the thing is coming-in and not going out. The meter is very useful in selecting and promoting bureaucrats, as only the people who can top the ratings will be having the biggest slots. It will also be handy in the parliament as members would be taking each other's readings and deciding the corresponding portfolios.

This family of meters will have products such as Satta-Meter. Just as Pakistani cricket team is heading for the field and innocent (stupid) people are crying and praying for its success, the Pakistani captain would be inserted Satta-Meter. The meter would reveal the real "scoop". The public can then stop praying and start bidding on the winning sides like Zimbabawe or Canada.

It is however important to sterilize all such equipment before the next use. It is also important to make sure the party has returned the meter back, as it is Pakistan and once things are taken-in...

LOSER-FRIENDLY GPS:

We want to give each person a hand-held device that will at least give him a fair chance in life. The looser Chuqandar would then blame the calculator instead of his screwed up Muqaddar.

What we are talking about here is just a plain probability GPS. Say you live in the orphan city of Karachi; your bhai jaan has severe toothache and needs to be taken to the dentist in Saddar. You will just input the origin and destination in the GPS and the reason for this adventure. Our GPS would be designed by smart-ass people (not the Telugu speaking H-1s) and will be totally loser-friendly with outputs like "Jaloos Main Pathrao Ka Imkaan Hai!!", "Aik dafa main suna karo!" and "Phir takleef??...Aaj calculations band hai!!"etc.

Hence the gadget would process all local parameters such as sniper firings, police stoppages, FBI picking, cars snatchings, bomb-blasts, buses/mini-buses storming, trucks turning turtle, bottom-less manholes (I don't mean the bay-area ones), fallen live wires, stray dogs, carbon mono-oxide breathing and garbage dumps, and would calculate the probability of survival as 3 out of 200. On the other hand, survival chances with toothache would be like 51 out of 100. So Bhai Jaan should stay home and give thanks on saving four other lives besides his.

SRI LANKAN DESSERT

It was July '87 and I was in Sri Lanka. Why? Well, I was there to buy coconut seeds and import them for my agricultural farm in Karachi.

The final exams were going on when I got instructions from my dad to proceed to Colombo. Even though father had given me a tight budget to work with, mom had given me some extra cash "just in case".

I got to Colombo via Air Lanka and asked the cabby to take me to a hotel close to everything as I needed the GPO (to call Karachi everyday), a taxi stand, a bus stand, etc. He took me to a building called Ceylinco hotel on Janadipathi Mawatha or "President Road". Later I realized that at that place everything was "Janadipathi" as the Presidency was close by. I saw "Janadipathi newspapers", "Janadipathi hairdresser", "Janadipathi dry cleaners", etc. Janadipathi was equivalent to "Presidential".

Ceylinco was kind of a 3.45 star hotel. I got an OK room with a nice view. As soon as I checked-in, I dashed to the dining lounge as it was 9:00 and I was starving. Since I was single, I took a seat at a dimly lit table for two which had a panoramic ocean view. Suddenly,

Sri Lankan Dessert

it started dawning on me. So here is Fakhri bhai...on a business trip, dining in a hotel lounge on the 7th floor with an open view of the Indian Ocean. Wow! This was overwhelming...Fakhri Bhai on 7th floor with an English menu!! Wah Beta Wah!

The entrees were listed all in English with somewhat Sinhalese calligraphy. I tried to get a hang of the menu...Shrimp Watta, Chicken and Kailay Ka Patta, Fish Khatta or Khatoonga or Fish Khatna. I ordered Fish Khatna! There came a plate with fish the size of shrimp on a heap of leafs and coconut powder smelling like the ocean. Price...Rs. 200. I looked up angrily at the Indian Ocean and suddenly found a waiter smiling at me curiously. Then he signaled a man in a black tux who came towards me. "Sir, my name is Diyabalangayand I am the manager guest relations. Is there anything I can do for you?"

This was kind of sudden as I wanted to take my wallet out under the table and see how much money I would be left minus 200. I stammered at first and then tried an old face saving technique. This is what I could utter out. "I want a sweet dessert". The manager looked amused and remarked: "All our desserts are sweet. Which one would you like?"

I had gathered myself by that time and demanded: "What do you have?" He retorted mechanically, "Caramel Mudslide, Pineapple Tsunami, Banana Hurricane..." Never heard of these before but I wanted to be even with him and make-up for my stammering. I tried to play it like Bond – Martini, Shaken Not Stirred! I asserted, "Not the usual stuff Mr. manager! Is there a dessert that I would really enjoy and that could satisfy me? After all, I am a foreign guest!"

He looked into my eyes. "What age are you as you look too young to order dessert and how long have you been ordering desserts?" OK, now that was plain insulting...Who does he think I am? Am I a kid who doesn't even know what hotel menus look like or may be I don't have money to pay for it?? I told him that I am 20 and a Computer Engineer and am here on a business trip from Pakistan.

This changed his looks. He smiled for the first time and asked me "Sir, why don't you order something that is a Sri Lankan delight!! It's called "Janadipathi Coconuts" or "Presidential Coconuts". It's a choice of business travelers like you! I though about it for a second..Ahh...imagine...coconut tasting fillings with fruit, custard, and jelly...like a sweet heaven. In those days, Feerni and Halwa were vanishing from Karachi dinners and Fruit Trifle was quickly becoming popular. Or even better...whispered my sweet tooth...Fruit Trifle filled in big creamy coconut shells...now I can brag as much I want to my friends and likes in Karachi...

I swallowed my saliva quickly and nodded yes. Mr. Diyabalangy, the manager, who was looking at me all this time came near and, with a victorious smile, told me: "It will be about 1000 Rupees". I swallowed one more time, this time in such a manner that the manager wouldn't notice. In a fraction of second, I calculated, Sri Lankan 1000 = Pak Rs. 500. So part of the money that mom gave me "just in case" will be going towards the dessert.

It was too late for me to say no. For one, I had "emergency" budget and Second, the honor and dignity of Pakistani businessmen was at stake. I "tried" to smile at him and said "It better be good". The manager didn't waste a second and called someone to get the "Janadipathi Coconuts". I asked him why you have to call someone to get it. He explained that they don't carry it all the time and it has to be fetched from downtown when a customer orders. He asked me what types of desserts are my favorites. Somehow, Gulab Jamun jumped into my mind. I told him that my favorite ones are soft, sweet and warm, the browner - the tastier! The Sinhalese fellow looked ecstatic.

Sri Lankan Dessert

"Oh yes", I added, "My sweet threshold is pretty high, usually the desserts feel flat to me" I smiled again giving off the looks of a confident young entrepreneur. The manager immediately called someone and told him to add "sweetness" to the dessert.

Several minutes passed and I was getting anxious. The hotel sound system was playing Jazz tunes. I heard a friendly whistle from Mr. Diyabalangay. The manager used his hands to show me the size of the coconuts found in the dessert. Ahh! Right then, I smelled a fragrance announcing the arrival of the dessert. I looked up impatiently and behold! The Sri Lankan Dessert walked right up to me and took the opposite chair. That was the one time in my life when I forgot both English and Urdu.

The manager was grinning from ear to ear. Rubbing his hands he winked at me: "I told you...you can't handle Sri Lankan Desserts". A drooling waiter slammed a bottle on my table "Take this dessert spoon to your room". Its label read something like "Mendes Dry Gin". The dessert then realized that something is not right as I am giving away "diabetic" looks. It exchanged some hot Sinhalese with the manager cursing him for not checking this customer's Sugar level beforehand.

Mr. Diyabalangay disappeared behind the counter and the dessert had to be returned while the packaging was still intact. Two waiters came for "consolation" to my table and whisked away the whiskey. Couple of folks on the other tables gave me pathetic looks that this Pakistani youngster was trying to go berserk as soon as he left his country, but thank God, the hotel management controlled the situation.

I don't remember how I reached my room. Checked out the next morning!!

TUSSI AARAHAY HO KAY JA RAHAY HO

I want to share some of the stories that my father used to tell me from his PIA days. He had his own way of telling tales and I used to listen enchanted.

FAUJ HAI ANDROONAY DARIYA:

Major General Iskander Mirza's son (I believe Humayun Mirza) was pushed to become Wing. Cmdr. when his father became the President, in spite of the fact that he used to "Stammer" big time. Then one fine morning, he was leading a formation of 5 F-86s Sabers on a training mission. The formation was to follow commands from the leader and not to do "anything" unless ordered.

Humayun Mirza chose to do a low level dive underneath a Bridge (Pul) on Jhelum river and then do a sudden vertical pull after to show his mastery. Wing Commander Mirza initiated the dive with the formation following. Then he pulled his fighter jet up just in time to avoid crashing into the river. The brilliant formation leader had to now give the order to the following Sabers to do the same.

According to my father, this is what PAF base Sargodha and the formation heard..."Poo Poo...Poo Poo Poo..Pull...Poo Poo...Abey Pul

Hai Pull...Damn it...Poo Poo Pull..."

Unfortunately, the four fighters crashed into Jhelum during the fifth Poo Poo. This event marks the biggest loss of Pakistan Air Force during peace time.

Mirza continued as Wing Commander until his father was ousted. He was the transferred to PIA. He stayed in PIA for sometime, but then took voluntary retirement. One of the reasons could be the things that people used to call him like "Pull Pull Mirza", "Admiral", "Sanu Nahar Walay Pul Tay Bula Kay!"

TUSSI AARAHE HO KAY JAA RAHE HO:

Those were the early PIA days and PIA had acquired the first Boeing 707. An Air Marshall had just taken over PIA and was eager to fly a jet liner. One day he arranged for himself to fly a maiden (no passenger) flight from Tehran to Karachi on the new Jet. My father had the Honor (Horror) to be in the cockpit as the flight engineer. A senior PIA pilot was there as the Co-Pilot, just in case.

The flight went eventless as Air Marshall was taking directions from the Co-Pilot. Then they entered Pakistan air space near Makran and contacted Karachi control tower for approach instructions. By now, it was night and the sky was dark. Air Marshall took the headset and opened the communications channel. A voice appeared on the radio receiver "This is Karachi, please come in, This is Karachi, please come in!" Air Marshall took a deep breath and with a victorious smile chuckled "Good Night Control Tower, this is PK123!". A voice came thru the receiver "Good Night PK123, Khuda Hafiz" and the radio went dead.

My father used to say that there was an aghast in the cockpit. Then he realized the mistake. Air Marshall had said "Good Night Control Tower", instead of "Good Evening Control Tower." As electronic communications were not as advanced in those days, the controller thought this is an outbound flight leaving Pakistan air space and discontinued communication.

Well, another channel was opened and luckily this time, people other than the Air Marshall, talked to the control tower. PK123 made a safe landing. The tower controller was suspended.

BEIJING...WE HAVE A PROBLEM:

This story took place when my father was stationed in Beijing. General Yahya Khan made a dash to Beijing to discuss the current (Voltage) situation in East Pakistan with Chinese leaders. My father's duty was to receive the VVIP aircraft and make sure all the technical formalities were taken care of.

All the hosts, including Chinese Premiers, dignitaries, protocol officers, embassy staff from a dozen countries, and the general public were waiting on the ground. Red carpet was laid on the runway to welcome the honored guests. Boys and Girls with flower bouquets were waiting and bands were playing tunes, etc. Then, the PIA plane appeared on the horizon. There was a cheer and roar on the ground and everyone was excited. The plane descended towards the runway, but then midway, it suddenly pulled up. The crowd had it's eyes and mouths wide open. The bands stopped. The aircraft gained some height and then started circling the airport. My father dashed to the control tower.

He was allowed to talk to the Pilot who reported that they were experiencing "some" problem and will land as soon as it's "fixed". The crew said that the President of Pakistan will not be able to attend the reception and arrangements should be made to escort him out of the airport ASAP. This was conveyed to the nervous Chinese who acknowledged. The plane landed after 10 minutes and stopped way back for lack of fuel. General Yahya was escorted out of the plane, with the help of two army officers, put in a black limo, and whisked away.

My father ran up the flight stairs in one breath and reached the cockpit. The captain was wiping sweat out of his face. When he looked at my father, he said "Susray Ko Patloon Pahna Rahe They". General Yahya had gotten drunk during the flight and threw away his pants. The army officers and the crew were trying to put his pants back on him. According to the Military code of uniform, a general cannot appear in public without his pants.

CHOP THE AIRLINES:

This story is related to the times when we still had East Pakistan. PIA was operating with Super Conies (Propeller aircraft) and was yet to acquire jet liners. One flight used to operate Karachi-Decca-Karachi and was a good means for people smuggling Paan, Pineapples, and Coconuts, and Bananas etc. into West Pakistan. The Air Marshall had taken over as Chairman of PIA.

On one such flight from Dhaka, "yaar log" loaded too many bananas into the cargo bay of the plane. As a result, it couldn't take-off and, after skidding, ditched into the unpaved ground besids the runway. The rain made the ground even softer and part of the plane sank into the earth. The report of the incident was telexed to Karachi. The Air Marshall gave it a deep thought and ordered that the plane be cut into pieces, chopped and removed from the runway without wasting time. This is necessary in order to keep the runway open for Pak Air Force operations, in case India attacks East Pakistan. This reply put the crew at Decca in a grave situation. Commander East Pakistan Rifles was contacted, a long thought was given and then a letter was sent back to Air Marshall as follows.

Chairman PIAC,
Karachi Airport.

Dear Sir,

PIA has only three Super Conies. Chopping one would mean losing 1/3rd airline. This would also end all air links between East Pakistan and West Pakistan. Also, this chopping would result in the termination of jobs for half of the airline employees. Further, we have confirmed that Pakistan Air Force has no aircrafts in East Pakistan. So, keeping in mind the families of half of the airline employees, please reconsider your decision.

P.S: The plane has been lifted out of the ground by using balloon jacks and is airworthy. This letter is being sent by the same plane, as Telex machine at Karachi is out of order.

PIA Staff,
Dhaka Airport.

UNITED ISLAM

The year is 20XX and finally Islam has shown it's dominance to the world. All the Islamic leaders are meeting in...New York...to announce Islamic Khilafah and a united Islam.

This will be broadcasted to the world in a show of Islamic pomp-glory and what else can better accomplish this other than a prayer under one Imam. That Imam could be the 1st Khalifah as well...the whole world is watching while holding its breath.

The organizers of this great event made arrangements for Fajar prayer to be broadcasted live from every channel in the world. All the Muslim heads-of-the-states agreed that Fajar prayer is impossible to make so let's all pray the Zuhar prayer under one Imam and let the world see a demonstration of united Muslim Ummah. Pakistan is invited to lead the prayer as the Islamic world's most populous country and the sole nuclear power state.

As soon as the Pakistani Imam accepted the honor, the Saudi delegation burped loudly and then retorted: "We cannot bray behind a Bakistani because Bakistanis don't Bray good, Blus they are Miskeens, Wallahi...Blus we follow Imam Al-Shafia...Blus all Bakistanis are Boor Beoble!!" Before Pakistanis could answer, the

Saudi king handed a fat envelope to the Pakistanis which quickly resolved the dispute and Pakistani stepped back.

Before the next Imam could be announced, the Taliban delegation threatened to blow them up if the Imam's beard does not pass the jar test. The Taliban leader brought an open ended jar and put it first on the Saudi king's chin for the length of beard test. This resulted in an exchange of Arabic & Pashtu language delicacies. After failing the test, the jar was tried on Qatari, Bangladeshi, Indonesian and Sudanese presidents and failed altogether. Then the Taliban leader victoriously jumped-up on the table and put the jar on his own chin. This resulted in an instant objection from the female Turkish premier as she thought that she is not getting a fair chance to compete in the jar test.

The Malaysian prime minister suggested having the Somali president as the Imam. The Syrians & Jordanians laughed, "We need more light in the hall Brazers, if this Ajwa Tamoor is going to be the Imam! Ha Ha Ha". This resulted in an outrage by the Sudanese, Somali, Ethiopian and Tanzanian delegates. The Kuwaiti Sheikh stood-up from his chair and offered each country 100 Million Khilafah currency which made them shut-up immediately.

By this time, the press was getting impatient. The CNN, Reuters and the now defunct Fox News reps. were anxious to get the footage of the 1st Islamic Khilafah prayers and show it to the world. Since Al-Jazeerah was now the official state media, only they were allowed to be close to the participants. Poor Geo News correspondents were thrown out of the conference as one reporter tried to ask the real age of the Egyptian president.

Lebanese president came forward and announced that I offer myself to be the Imam. I am diverse as my Parents were Muslim, Jews and Christian from time to time. Palestinian president offered to be the Moazzin as he is from the 74th branch of Islam. That seemed to be a good idea till the Palestinian president took out a piece of paper and started reading Aza'an. The Pakistani prime minister declared such Aza'an as void and the Afghan premier revolted against a Lebanese Imam as they eat Jhatka and most probably drink alcohol. The UAE Sheikh was surprised as what was wrong in that.

The Bengali president tried to cool down the situation and called the Pakistani president to "Shit Down". The Lebanese group said "Thank You!" and he replied "Shame to You!" This did not help much and the Pakistanis shouted "Bhooka Bengali". The Kuwaiti premier turned-on his earpiece and asked "Wallahi! What is Bhooka?" It took more than 30 minutes for the staff to explain "Bhooka" to the Kuwaiti head-of-state and by this time it was almost the time for Asar prayer.

A CNN correspondent, who had recently taken Shahadah impressed by the glory of united Islam, shouted that he is a new Muslim and he can lead the prayer. The Saudis and the Gulf sheikhs were delighted on the idea of being lead by an American. However, the Algerians protested that they would prefer a French convert to lead the prayer. The Indonesians wanted a Dutch Imam and the Africans Muslims revolted for a British convert. Pakistanis opined that as long as it's a white guy, that's all it counts. Also, whoever gives the most donations for the flood victims can also lead the prayer.

Embarrassed, the conference administrators, got hold of a white guy whose father was an American and mother French. He had studied in Holland and accepted Islam in Britain. He could speak English, French, Arabic and Dutch. Everybody was so happy that at last united Islam can pray the Zuhar prayer...at Maghrib time. Prayer timings were not important...what was important was the united Islam...

As soon as the Imam stepped-up on the Musallah...a voice cracked the silence. "This prayer cannot proceed!" Everyone looked at the Iranian president. "This Imam has all the qualities of a Western agent! Marg Bar West!". There was another poetic exchange among the Musalleen in English, Arabic, Persian, Bangla and Urdu with Pashtu slogans and Chinese and French translations.

The time now is 1:00 AM. The world media is watching the first united Islam Zuhar prayer. Subhanallah, 55 Imams are leading the Prayer, most without a single person behind them...everyone is crying the tears of joy...the day has finally arrived...

ZAROORAT-E-JAHEZ

Zaroorati Ailan Samaat Farmaiye!

Hamaray Barkhurdar Kay Liye Achay Jahez Walay Rishtay Ki Zaroorat Hay.

Rishtay Ki Shakal Jaisi Bhi Ho...Jahez Ki Shakal Achi Ho.

Hum Zaat-Paat, Khandaan, Baraadari, Rang-o-Nasal Jaisi Khurafaat Pay Yaqeen Nahin Rakhtay...Sirf Jahzez Pay Rakhtay Hain.

Pahlay Aaeeye Pahlay Laeeye Ki Bunyad Pay.

Allah Ka Diya Sab Hay Izzat Kay Siwa...

Larka Amreeka Main Pahlay Hi Settled Hay...Aur Na Sirf Green Card Rakhta Hay Balkay Soccer Main Yellow, Red Card Waghera Bhi Mil Jatay Hain!

Larka Zihanat (Chalaaki) Main Abba Pay Gaya Hay Aur Shakal Main Amma Pay (Shukar Hay)

Larkay Ki Amma Doctor Hay Aur Abba Bhi Kuch Kartay Hai

Hum Larkon Ki Shadi Pay Itna Jahez Jama Karna Chahtay Hain Kay Larkiyon Ki Shadi Pay Usi Main Say Tika Dain...

Hum Larkon Ki Shadi Pay Itna Jahez Jama Karna Chahtay Hain Kay Larkiyon Ki Shadi Pay Usi Main Say Tika Dain...

Cash, Credit Card Aur Certified Check Walay Foran email Karen...Udhaar, Personal Check Ya Laaray-Lappay Walay Hazrat Koi Aur Ghar Dhoonden...

Larka Mashallah Aik Hafta Pahlay Teen Ager Ho Gaya Hay...Laikin Teen Ki Cheezen Jahez Main Na Dain...

Hum CSS Kar Kay "Na Jaiz" Amadni Nahin Chahtay...Sirf Jahez Waghera Ki Jayez Amadni Chahtay Hain...

Larkay Kay Kamanay Say Ziyada Aham Yeh Hay Kay Larkee Walay Kiya Kamatay Hain...

An Equal Opportunity In-Lawyer...

THE END

www.ingramcontent.com/pod-product-compliance
Lightning Source LLC
Chambersburg PA
CBHW071706040426
42446CB00011B/1946